Letters from Ghana

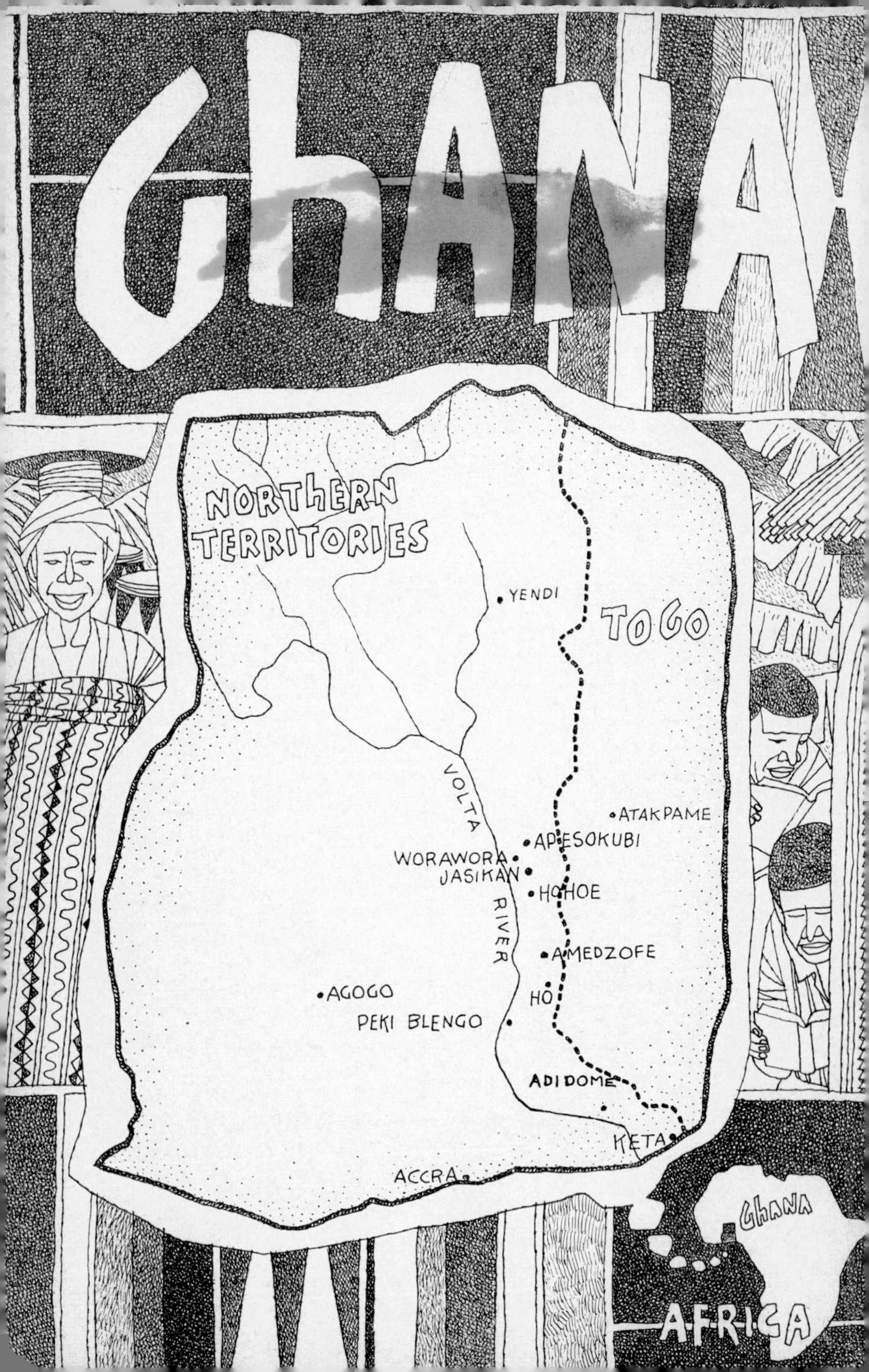
GHANA
NORTHERN TERRITORIES
YENDI
TOGO
VOLTA RIVER
ATAKPAME
APESOKUBI
WORAWORA
JASIKAN
HOHOE
AMEDZOFE
HO
AGOGO
PEKI BLENGO
ADIDOME
KETA
ACCRA
GHANA
AFRICA

Letters from Ghana

by Richard and Gertrude Braun

Photographs by Stanley Wilke

The Christian Education Press

Philadelphia

Library of Congress Catalog Card No.: 59-12710

Editor's Foreword

It started on March 6, 1957. That was the day that Dr. and Mrs. Richard C. Braun landed in Ghana to begin their first term of medical missionary service abroad. That was also Independence Day for Ghana. The date is now printed across the face of many of the stamps issued by that country.

So just as the Gold Coast became the new independent nation of Ghana, Dick and Trudy Braun landed at Accra and joined in the festivities. This was such an interesting period in history that these young medical missionaries sent from the Evangelical and Reformed Church to serve through Ghana's indigenous Evangelical Presbyterian Church had much to write home about. Their excitement seems the most natural thing in the world. They were off on an unknown adventure in a brand-new nation in West Africa. They brought with them a Doctor of Medicine degree recently earned by Dick, a Registered Nurse degree earned by Trudy, their young son Kenneth, and a world of confidence and hope in the mission that their Christian faith had sent them on.

Under these circumstances they poured out their thoughts freely in letters sent home to their parents. It should be noted that these letters were not written for publication. Perhaps this accounts for much of the spontaneity that abounds in the following pages.

The Africa that Dick and Trudy Braun present in this collection of letters is part of what has been called "the continent of the future." It is that part of the world where things are happening with amazing speed. And nowhere is this more true than in Ghana, one of the newest nations in Africa.

The African scenes that flash before the reader's eye in this book vibrate with a living quality that comes from viewing something new from a fresh perspective. Fortunately, both of the Brauns have a lively literary style as well as a sharp reportorial eye. But most of the power of these letters comes not from a skillful method of expression but from the realities that these young people grappled with. Both are extremely capable persons—interesting, resourceful, and dedicated. As a doctor and nurse medical team, they were called upon to face the ultimate issues of life and death in a strange land. As their story unfolds, the reader may feel that he is reading about all missionaries who ever left home, family, and loved ones to serve their fellow men in an overseas land. The writing is vivid, spontaneous, and powerful. But more than that, it is so intimately personal that it is truly universal.

JAY FUSSELL

Letters from Ghana

Accra, Ghana
March 7, 1957

Dear Folks:

We're here! We still find it hard to believe. But one of these days we'll probably wake up to the fact that after looking forward and preparing for this event for years, at last we've arrived. It's wonderful to be in Ghana!

But where to start this report? The new nation of Ghana? Air trip? First impressions of Accra? There's so much to tell; we'll probably be using up quite a few air letters. Guess we'll start with the trip.

Monday morning in London dawned early and foggy—the foggiest we've seen. We were worried that the Vicar who was seeing us off, would not be able to find the air terminal. Then we ran almost smack into it. We were two hours late in taking off, and then it was only after transferring to another airport twenty-five or thirty miles out that we were finally able to get away. From then on we had a wonderful trip and enjoyed it all. The independent airline on which we flew is severely restricted by the government in order to avoid competition with its state-supported counterpart. As a result, it is allowed to run only third-class flights in older planes that cruise at 180 miles per hour. But to us it seemed first-class all the way!

The plane was a two-engine, ten-year-old Viking carrying twenty-two passengers and a crew of five. It was not pressurized, so had to fly at 9,000 feet. We saw therefore much of the passing country. It was a bit noisy, but we sailed smoothly without much vibration. The crew was helpful and friendly; excellent food was served every two or three hours.

After crossing the English Channel we watched the flat patchwork squares of France go by. Once we caught a glimpse of lovely Bordeaux, and later we stopped for lunch at Biarritz. The clouds hid much of Spain and also Gibraltar. We landed in Tangiers, which was an interesting sight with its contrasts of beautiful new buildings and tottering hovels, of women in purdah and others decidedly not. We spent the night in a modern hotel with private bath. (Did that shower feel good!)

Tuesday we skirted the African coast. French Morocco is fertile, like France; but the Spanish Sahara was the most God-forsaken country we've seen. At Bathurst we saw for the first time Black Africa: luxuriant growth, friendly people, grass huts (one with a Singer sewing machine in front), and the British colonial system. We stayed in a brand-new seaside hotel where during the night we had to use blankets to keep warm. In Freetown we had another delicious lunch. Next stop was Takoradi, a bustling, prosperous little town, all decked out in flags for the birth of Ghana. An atmosphere of proud achievement prevailed everywhere. It was then only a forty-minute hop to Accra, the end of our trip. We were sorry to leave the friends we had made during the flight.

Kenny was a good little trouper; but he was pretty sick for two days with an unexplained fever as high as 105 degrees on Tuesday. We could not find anything wrong except for the fever and listnessness. We finally concluded it was immature mechanism for acclimatization. He had not yet learned to drink more water, and increased sweating had not yet started. It was interesting to observe, for I had never heard of that before except in an outright heat stroke. He is fine now, and already drinking water by the gallon.

Customs at the airport did not cause too much delay, considering the immigration forms we had to fill out. Some of our English fellow passengers were irritated by the delay, which they attributed to African inefficiency. When it came our turn we tried to show a little friendliness. When they saw why we came, the chief clerk drew up proudly and gave us a rousing, "Ghana Welcome You!" That brought lumps to our throats. We realized what a momentous occasion the coming of independence is for the people here, and indeed for the whole world. If more people would realize what a privilege it is to help these people, there would be more welcome mats extended. But there is no evidence anywhere of bitterness because of the past. Although some of the missionaries were apparently a little fearful of race riots and outbreaks of violence, the whole Independence celebration has been carried out with dignity.

Here in Accra we are staying at the mission rest house as guests of Dr. Ned Moser, his wife Alice, and their children: Janice, four, and Danny, two. It is in the same area with the Scottish missionaries' homes and will be our home whenever we come to Accra for supplies. We've spent most of our time asking questions (there's so much to learn) about buying supplies, how to stay well, how to work septic tanks, kerosene refrigerators, gasoline generators, how to get along with African help, and so forth. Tomorrow we buy supplies, open a bank account, register at the U.S. Embassy and Medical

Department. It's been very comfortable here, about 84 degrees, with a good breeze always. Sleeping is not difficult, especially during siestas.

The plan is for us to tour the section of Ghana where our mission stations are located and thus get acquainted with our church's work. Then we will make our way to Worawora, where we will be stationed for about five months helping Dr. Moser while Dr. Christfried Doering is away on furlough.

↙ ↙ ↙

Adidome, Ghana
March 10, 1957

It is 8:30 in the morning. For half an hour already the children have been filing past the door on their way to Sunday school. There was no Sunday school a year and a half ago when Mrs. Whitcomb came, but now over sixty children come. I must go over to hear that singing and see those children dressed in togas or long white dresses. Dick is making hospital rounds with Dr. Whitcomb. We are to observe the work here for three days, especially the construction of the hospital where we hope to carry out our life work.

But first, back to Accra. We did not finish telling you about it in our last letter. It was a thrill to arrive in Ghana on the very day it became an independent nation. The town was beautifully decorated for the celebration with the red, green, and yellow flags everywhere and decorations on the streets where the dignitaries traveled. Here there is a beautiful memorial arch in the best English style of architecture, bearing the words *Freedom and Justice.*

Thursday morning we drove around the town and then out

to Achimota, where they were having a big durbar (or meeting of the chiefs) for the Duchess of Kent. We did not have tickets. But since the Worawora hospital's Chevy ranch wagon is the same shade of green as the whole fleet of new Chevies for the VIP's, we were ushered straight through the crowds to the official parking lot and walked right in. There was a big field, on one side of which was the "reviewing stand." Lining the other sides were many Ghana chiefs and their retinues of drummers, umbrella-carriers, and official hangers-on. The huge brightly-colored umbrella is the mark of a chief. When the Duchess arrived, preceded by a parade of colorful horsemen and two bands (one African, one English), all the chiefs crossed the field one at a time and each with his full retinue to be presented. Ned Moser and Dick tried to look important and walked right up to the stand. They did get some good pictures, but soon they were evicted for not being official press photographers.

Accra is, in part, a modern city with many new buildings of modern design. Half the city seems to be owned by two rival trading companies—Union Trading Company, a Swiss company, with origins in the old Basel Mission, and United Africa Company, a subsidiary of Lever Brothers. The latter has a brand-new department store, called Kingsway, with everything from frozen foods to Arrow shirts. Just about everything is now available in Accra. But canned goods, the staple diet of missionaries, are expensive—up to fifty cents for a can of vegetables. So the cost of living is quite high.

Besides these large stores, there are countless stalls and shops and street sellers with everything from trinkets to native foods. The markets are filled with colorfully dressed Africans, the women carrying babies on their backs plus a full load on their heads and in their hands. It's amazing they don't drop something. Shopping for the missionaries is a headache, for when anyone goes to Accra he gets lists from all the missionaries round about as well as a full list of hospital needs. Our list has everything from chamber pots to coffin nails.

The Scottish Mission Press in Accra is really a going affair with a large attractive bookstore. It is the largest print shop in Accra and is more than self-supporting.

In Accra we saw autos of American, English, and German make. We also saw many mammy-lorries, about which we had heard so much. They are the big trucks used as buses all over the country. They have brightly-painted slogans on the back, many of them religious.

Of course Accra has slums, and some of them are quite filthy and stinky. I am sure the Duchess of Kent was never taken to see them. Here one finds open sewers, people bathing in the streets, and naked children and adults. On one trip Dick saw his first leper. Ned and Dick met the chief of Worawora on the street; he did not look nearly so impressive without his umbrella, his stool, his retinue, and drummers.

Ned and Dick went to the main government hospital to talk over the tuberculosis program with their specialist, who seemed to be quite interested in having the government aid Worawora in setting up a tuberculosis clinic. Medical registration with the health department was no problem, since they already had all the credentials. We had dinner at the airport and saw Nixon's huge Air Force plane fly over.

I think the hardest thing for us to get used to is having a servant at our constant call. Apparently the Africans are having a little trouble adjusting to the fact that they are free and don't have to yield constantly to the whites.

WE ARE NOW in Ho, but we haven't told you much about
Adidome. It is eighty miles from Accra, the first sixty-five
miles being excellent blacktop highway on which we rolled
along at seventy miles per hour. There was little traffic. The
country was desolate, almost completely wasteland.

Then we hit the Volta River and the ferry, which was a
decrepit old barge pushed by an old launch. There was a line
of about six mammy-lorries waiting, but they ushered us ahead
and we managed to squeeze on along with a lorry filled with
Africans. Along the bank we saw many children swimming.
Their mothers were washing the clothes and then filling their
water jugs and walking off with the huge jugs on their heads.
The river is not very wide at this point, only about half a mile,
but it carries a lot of water and looks quite clear in the dry
season. The last twelve miles was a terrible gravel road; then
we found ourselves in Adidome. To say that it was not quite
what we expected would be an understatement. It reminded
us of parts of southern Texas with broad flat expanses of
wasteland, little vegetation, few trees, and mostly just dry
grass. Certainly no jungle around here! It's a sparsely popu-
lated area; but there are quite a few villages around, with mud
huts and grass roofs.

We drove up to the Whitcombs' house which was all decked
out with U.S. and Ghana flags. It was good to see them and
spend three days in their home. We know we are going to
enjoy working with them. We were amazed at how comfortably they live in their African-style home made of mud with a
tin roof. It has been nicely white-washed and cleaned up.

They have no electricity—but then they go to bed soon after dark. They get most of their water from the river one quarter of a mile away, but use filtered and boiled rain water for cooking and drinking. Their kerosene refrigerator is very efficient. Dr. Whitcomb built a septic tank and put in a toilet that is flushed by pouring a bucket of water into it. They take baths by pouring water over themselves—strictly African fashion. All their furniture is made locally of beautiful mahogany (even packing crates and forms for concrete are made of mahogany).

The thing we liked most about the way they live is their closeness to the people. There are huts all around them. It was not long before children were swarming around Kenny on the veranda, and local women came to welcome Trudy. All the Africans are very friendly and the Whitcombs have a knack for making them feel welcome. It will be much more difficult to live close to the people in our new home set up on high pillars and located away from the village.

A large part of the hospital has already been built since the cornerstone laying in January. The buildings are not beautiful but they are efficient and cool. The hospital is on top of a gentle rise where there is always a good breeze. From this point we have a good view of the river to the south. The house being built for us would cost $25,000 in the States. It almost embarrasses us. There are three bedrooms, two baths, living room, dining room, study, kitchen, storeroom—all on one level on ten-foot concrete pillars. Underneath the house is a carport and lots of room for shaded play space. When the water system gets in, with pumps, there should be plenty of water for irrigation. They have already ordered two hundred fruit trees to help fill the two hundred acres given with the hospital ground.

Church was quite an experience Sunday morning. The primary school building has a tin roof and open sides. It was well filled with African adults and children, who were interested in looking at us. But since we sat in front, we could not look at them. The pastor repeated almost everything in English for the benefit of the Whitcombs and us, and then gave a résumé of the sermon. We have been waiting a long time to hear their singing; and it was worth it! The middle school children sang an anthem in really good four-part harmony. We were introduced and Dick had to make a little speech. Tuesday we visited the school and watched them play games and sing.

Tuesday was market day in Adidome, so we made the rounds of the stalls with Mrs. Whitcomb. Such an array of strange foods and odors we have never before experienced. Some of these foods should prove worth trying, especially the groundnuts and the yams. But we'll be content to leave most of them alone. We did buy a basketful of limes for eight cents.

So far, Africa is a fascinating place—even in the middle of the night when we hear drums in the distance.

⚶ ⚶ ⚶

Peki Blengo, Ghana
March 18, 1957

HERE WE ARE in a lovely little town between high hills, where it is always cool. But first we must tell you about Ho. We stayed there three days with the Al Schwenkes in their old mud house on stilts, built almost one hundred years ago by

German missionaries. They have no running water, but do have bucket latrines. In the evening there is electricity and it's quite comfortable.

Al is the treasurer of the Evangelical Presbyterian Church, which means that he goes on a seven-hundred-mile trek every month to pay the salaries of all the pastors and teachers of the three hundred schools run by the church. That payroll runs up to $80,000 a month. So the church here is big business. (This is entirely African; the mission funds are separate.) The secondary school in Ho—Mawuli (God with us)—is quite impressive with its modern buildings. We had a good time there with the David Desmonds. He is a teacher of physics and chemistry in the school and she is a nurse. One night we had dinner with Mrs. Vivian Hazel, who teaches home economics.

Here we were invited for dinner into the home of the Rev. Felix Buatsi, the Synod Clerk of the Evangelical Presbyterian Church. You remember he went to the United States as a fraternal delegate to the General Synod of the Evangelical and Reformed Church in 1956 and also attended our commissioning service in Chicago. We first met him at the Brauns in Webster Groves. Inviting missionaries to dinner was not done before he went to the States. His wife is charming. We met also several of his seven children. The meal was mostly African—a spicy noodle soup, then groundnut (peanut) soup with chicken (very good), then boiled yam. The yam here has no resemblance to ours at home. It is a white tuber about two or three feet long, weighing up to twenty-five pounds. This was served with cocoyam leaves, which taste very much like spinach. We find the African food quite palatable and we think we'll use it wherever possible. We are still looking forward to our introduction to fu fu.

In Ho, Dick went to the government offices and met the regional officer and his assistant, both of whom are English, and the highest officers in the Togoland area. They are very fine gentlemen. The regional officer even preaches in the churches occasionally, and in Ewe! Ho is hilly, more forested than Adidome, and more prosperous. The government is putting in a water system and an electricity system. We went through the government hospital and met the African doctor (just out of school) who is to take complete charge of the forty beds, plus one hundred outpatients daily. He is also expected to spend two full days at outlying clinics as much as fifty miles away. All previous English doctors at that hospital have had their health broken in a short time. He is getting his experience fast. In addition to the above responsibilities he cares for a leper colony of about 125 patients, which we visited. The colony is rather primitive, but apparently good work is done here.

At Peki Blengo, the Graus run the school for missionary children. There are ten at the moment, including their four, but twelve more potential scholars are on the way. Here Esther Mae Reimold has her headquarters for youth work; and there is a seminary for African catechists, taught by the Rev. Eugene Grau, the Rev. George Snyder, and the Rev. Mr. Ansre (African). The Snyders have a beautiful new home on the hillside, referred to as the "castle." They are almost due for retirement, having spent thirty years in China before being transferred to Ghana.

Yesterday morning in church Dick again had to make a speech. It is hard to keep a train of thought when you have to stop every sentence for translation. The people are very friendly. Since church we have had four delegations of visitors. The Rev. Mr. Ansre brought a live chicken, two paw-paws, and a lovely bunch of roses. About thirty women of the Bible class marched in a procession up the hill singing, one of them carrying on her head a huge tray with about five dozen bananas (Kenny has since reduced that number considerably). This morning a group of women brought another live chicken, four yams (about eighty pounds on one head!), and a dozen grapefruit. We were royally welcomed.

One of the reasons for these visits is plain, and points to the frustration that we will probably feel frequently. Across the valley can be seen four brand-new little concrete buildings which the townspeople built in the hope that God would provide them with a doctor. At present the buildings go unused except for the Ho doctor's visit once fortnightly. In addition a native midwife occasionally uses the buildings along with an African dispenser (provided by the government) whose knowledge and supply of drugs is extremely limited. One building has five rooms which would make a spacious clinic; another is built with two six-bed wards. There are also two small bungalows. It would be a good set-up for one doctor and nurse. Yesterday afternoon a delegation of five town leaders came to see us—three church elders, the chief's spokesman, and the Rev. Mr. Ansre—to plead that the American missionaries send them a doctor. They deserve one, as do many villages. But what can one say? Only encourage them.

Kenny is well, eats quantities of bananas, and drinks gallons of water.

Weighing in; this baby is one of 229 born in the Worawora hospital in 1958.

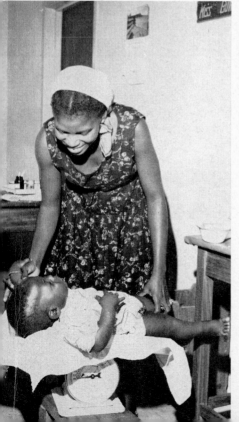

"Have you been taking your medicine regularly?" . . . Adidome hospital; Doctor Braun at times serves at Worawora.

Patient arriving at Adidome hospital for medical attention

Patient brings his prescription to the clerk in charge of Worawora hospital pharmacy.

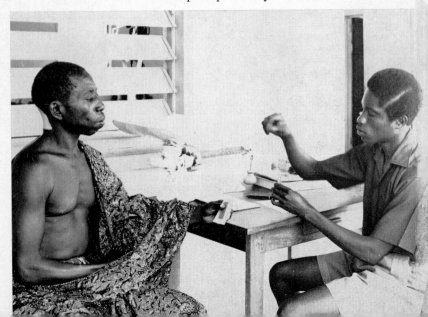

WHEN WE ARRIVED here in Worawora, we found our first letters from you waiting for us. They were sent from Oak Park, Webster Groves, and from Grinnell. It takes a week to ten days to get airmail letters from you. There are now three flights a week from Accra to the United States. Before Independence there was only one each week.

Here in Worawora we find ourselves in very lovely country that reminds us of Pennsylvania with its green, wooded hills. This is one of the most prosperous regions of Ghana. Cocoa is the chief crop. On our way here we saw a number of cocoa farms. We are now hoping to get a closer view of the trees and the produce during the present harvest season. The people seem very friendly too, though they are more sophisticated than the poorer ones around Adidome.

The Worawora hospital looks very prosperous with its nineteen modern, screened-in buildings. It's quite an institution. Each ward or functional unit, such as laundry, is housed in a separate building to take advantage of whatever breeze comes up the hospital hill. All the units, except doctors' homes and nurses' cottages, are connected by covered walks. The most obvious need here seems to be an intercom system. Too bad we can't understand the talking drums and set up a portable system like that.

The wards are very nice. Since they are completely screened, the need for mosquito netting over the beds is eliminated. We wonder whether the patients find it hard to go back to sleeping on mats after getting used to hospital beds. In the children's ward, one relative is allowed to stay each night with a child. But on rounds this week we found as many as three or four relatives sleeping on the floor beside each crib. That makes walking a bit difficult, so Mabel Burket cleared out all those above the allowed number. It is obvious that to try to staff this place with one doctor and three registered nurses (as at present) results in much overwork and inadequate use of facilities.

The house where we are staying with the Mosers is only a year old. It is both comfortable and modern, including a tiled bathroom. The only thing it lacks is hot running water; and there aren't too many times when one can't do without hot water in this climate. The wide screened verandas shade the walls of the house on the south and north and catch prevailing winds from the south. In the evening there is usually a cooling breeze that lasts until morning. The hottest time of day is from noon till three. Then everyone closes down for lunch and siesta.

Next week, after the Schlers leave for Accra, we will settle down in the Doering mansion for four months. We will be rattling around in five times as much space as we are used to, since there are three bedrooms, two baths, large living room, dining room, and kitchen. The veranda and cement space beneath the house will provide a wonderful play space for Kenny. We hear our extra bedroom will be put to frequent use, however, for the missionary's house is the usual stop for all Europeans[1] who come to Worawora. Last week the Mosers had a businessman stay with them a week without compensa-

---

[1] *European* in this sense is a term used by Africans to refer to any white person.

tion. It makes for good public relations but is a bit hard on the pocketbook.

The Schlers will fly home on April 2 (they are agricultural missionaries from Missouri, whom we met at Eden Seminary). Dan's infectious hepatitis has not responded too well to treatment. Both he and Mary need a rest. Whether in the United States or here, it will be hard for Dan to get the rest that is important for his recovery because he sees so many things that need to be done and has so many good ideas.

While Dan is away, he is leaving his flock of chickens and rabbits under the care of an African worker who is to get a share of them in return for his stewardship. We are buying a share of the rabbits too, so that we can build up a supply of fresh meat. It is almost a necessity for each family to have its own farm in order to insure a dependable supply of fruits and vegetables, not to mention eggs, which are very scarce. The best chickens are a cross of Rhode Island Reds and African bush hens.

Last evening the pastor of Worawora paid us a visit. He impressed us very favorably, as have the other African ministers. This pastor is in charge of thirteen parishes and supervises the work of evangelists carrying on pastoral duties in the individual churches. He is planning to arrange for one of the teachers in the middle school of the Evangelical Presbyterian Church to be our Ewe teacher. The synod has granted us the privilege of spending four months in language study before we move to Adidome to take the Whitcombs' place while they are on furlough. None of the other missionaries has been given this opportunity before being pressed into active duty, so we feel we must make full use of this chance. Unfortunately Ewe is not the language spoken in this area, so we won't be hearing it in the market place and at church. Our helpers, however, are Ewe people. We tell them that one of their duties is to help us learn the language. The hardest part of it will be to stay away from the hospital when we see the pressure of work there.

We are eager to see the write-up of Worawora in *The Messenger*. We promised our friends to write to the editor and see if there can't be a special Africa mailing. By the time the magazine gets here it is three months old. It's lucky the merit of the paper does not decrease with age.

Your "International Relations" club gift will be used to pay for two hundred citrus trees ordered for Adidome. We will be reaping some of the fruits and pleasures of the greenery.

✗   ✗   ✗

Worawora, Ghana
March 31, 1957

Is THAT DATE right? Where has March gone? It's been the shortest month of our lives! And this has been an especially busy week. Now that we have moved into the Doering mansion, we are trying to get settled in what seems to us a big house with lots of wide open spaces.

Last Sunday we attended the local church. The service was conducted in Twi and Dick had to make the customary speech. After church the pastor and the Mosers took us to meet the chief. We had an appointment, just to make it proper. The chief was waiting for us on his veranda, sitting on his official stool and surrounded by the stools of his elders (about a dozen). No one said much until everyone had arrived. Then, while we remained seated, all the elders came around in line to shake hands, without talking. They sat down and we went around shaking hands. That was repeated two or three times in the course of half an hour. Then the pastor formally introduced us and the spokesman for the elders welcomed us. Then there was some kind of palaver in Twi, during which the elder expressed dissatisfaction that at times there is just one doctor at Worawora. He was also unhappy that we would be leaving for Adidome. So Ned had to explain to them, apparently to their satisfaction.

After dinner on Sunday we set out for Accra on a shopping spree together with Mabel Burket and Tawia, our new houseboy. Mabel is releasing Tawia as her gardenboy and we are training him as a houseboy. The Chevy ranch wagon handled beautifully. We did the 170 miles in four and a half hours. The last half is all fairly new blacktop and we could roll along at 65 miles per hour. We went over the new Volta Bridge, the picture of which you've probably seen. Agba, the hospital driver, drove the hospital two-ton lorry down, and then drove us around Accra and showed us where to go. We got a little better feeling of the city than last time when we were struck by the great contrast between the modern new buildings and the conditions of squalor.

We went hog-wild on the buying. We spent £98 (or $270) mostly on food, buying by the case on some things like Heinz tomato soup and baked beans, and Kellogg's cornflakes. The trouble is that you don't save a farthing by buying in quantity. If you buy a case of twenty-four cans, the check-out girls just ring it up twenty-four times! And they have small size containers, as in England. You don't buy sugar in greater than two-pound boxes, or soap in anything but small boxes. Almost everything is available there with most of the famous U.S.

brands plus English, French, Swiss, Dutch, and German brands. But everything is very expensive. A No. 2½ can of tomatoes costs 38 cents; a No. 2 can of grapefruit juice, 28 cents; and a dozen eggs, $1.04. Everybody uses huge quantities of Kool-aid, mostly because lemons aren't always available in the market. Many fruits and vegetables that grow readily here are not used by the Africans. So if we want them, we have to grow them ourselves. Their diet must be horribly monotonous, based almost entirely on yams, cassava, and plantains. One thing always available is bananas, and we eat our fill of them at eight for a nickel.

We spent some extra time in Accra looking around, walking through the government hospital, looking around the exclusive Ambassador Hotel as though we owned it, and had a wonderful swim in the Atlantic. We went to a movie and saw a terrible picture on "crime pays if done for the right reason."

We are now living in the Doering house. It's really incongruous to be living in this comfort when we are supposed to be primitive. The mission provides all the basic furniture except lamps and things like that. We will have three helpers— a gardenboy named Kumla, a houseboy named Tawia, and Nellie, whose job will be to look after Kenny and help cook. Total cost: $39.00 a month. It's hard getting used to having them around. We have to teach them everything; we can't take anything for granted. Tawia still carefully puts the caps back on empty coke bottles.

Yesterday we had our first Ewe lesson from Mr. Adzasi. He seems nice. We should have a good time if we can push ourselves to work at it for six hours a day. Our teacher is a middle school teacher who wants to apply classroom methods by starting out with grammar. But I guess he'll get used to the smaller, informal class. The Ewe alphabet has thirty phonetic letters. We are finding that the linguistics we had at the missionary conference at Meadville is a real aid in helping us understand that much at least, even though we can't distinguish some of the sounds as yet.

Kenny has been a real trouper through all the moving around. He still likes to keep one of us in sight whenever possible and will bring his book or plaything and plop down right in the middle of what we are doing. He and the cat, Rackety, seem to enjoy each other immensely. We have to keep an eye on Kenny so he doesn't drop food on the floor on purpose, or swipe the cat's food for himself. Our helpers are so willing to do things for Kenny, like picking up his toys or carrying him, because it is easier and faster than waiting for him to walk. We have to remind them to let him do things for himself.

All our stuff came through well, with only about five dollars breakage (mostly our good glasses). Some clothes were mildewed, but we think that happened in the St. Louis August weather rather than en route. Wish you were here to enjoy the gentle cool breeze.

⚲ ⚲ ⚲

Worawora, Ghana
April 7, 1957

OUR FIRST HOUSE GUEST here is Dr. Whitcomb, who came last Tuesday after seeing the Schlers off at Accra. He and Ned Moser have been spending every morning doing the elective surgery that Ned has been scheduling for the past couple of months. Most operations, such as hernia, have been done with local anesthesia. That seems incongruous in that fancy operating room. The only alternative is drop ether, which certainly isn't the anesthesia of choice these days. In the evenings Dick and Dr. Whitcomb have been poring over medical supply catalogues and ordering instruments and essential equipment for the Adidome hospital. So far they've "spent" over $1,500—but that is only a beginning. Of course, one of the things Dick wants most is a simple anesthesia machine and the stuff to give spinal anesthesia. It's a satisfaction for us to be in on the planning stage at Adidome, since that will be our home station.

We spent most of our non-study time last week getting things organized. Dick went down to the dispensary to familiarize himself with the drugs used here. Most of them were unfamiliar trade names. Now he plans to help in the clinic, seeing patients one or two hours a day. Trudy supervised the initial cleaning of the house and has worked out a regular schedule for our workers to follow through the week. What a new experience to say, "Please wax and polish the furniture and floors in this room, and clean the windows," and not have to do it yourself. I still have a guilty feeling in letting someone else do my work. But it does give the needed time for study and helping out in the hospital. Our houseboy, Tawia, seems to be very bright. Gradually I am teaching him to do some of the cooking. Baking bread is the next thing on the list. It was a luxurious feeling when we had a housewarming, with eleven for supper, not to have to do the cleaning up and dishwashing.

About five o'clock we went for a ride and stopped at the adobe house where the Whitcombs lived when they were here. That was a worthwhile stop. We found about twenty bananas on the mission tree and three pawpaws that are almost ripe.

The latter taste something like cantaloupes. The fruit on the mission trees disappears if not watched, so tomorrow we want to go and get the rest of the bananas and let them ripen here.

Kumla put in our garden this week. The very fertile ground on the hill behind the house is terraced with beans, corn, and tomatoes planted on the level spaces and groundnuts (peanuts to you) planted on the slopes to hold the soil. There is no shortage of space here, so planting is easy. You just dig holes, drop the seeds, and wait for the rainy season. It will be fun to see what develops. How we are longing for fresh vegetables. The only kinds we have are two kinds of greens that grow wild and are a fairly good substitute for spinach. We can buy bananas for about five cents a bunch, but we won't be able to pick them or the pineapple for about eighteen months after they are planted. Last Thursday, market day, we were lucky to find limes for sale. Usually they are hard to find because the people use them only for cleaning pots and don't think of marketing them. We have tipped off our helpers that we will take all the limes and fresh eggs that people will bring to market. Don't fear we won't be swamped. The eggs are very small; it takes two or three of them for each egg called for by a recipe.

The rainy season is due to begin soon now. We can expect an hour or two of rain every day, beginning at four. Clothing and books kept in a closed place will mold, but an occasional airing in the brilliant sunshine will remedy that. Even in the rainy season laundry is no problem, for the morning sun is very hot. The few rains we had this last week were very welcome, for they cooled the air and settled the dust on the road.

So far we have found the climate quite agreeable in Wora-wora—a great improvement over London. It begins to get light in the morning at about 5:30. Within an hour trucks and workers are climbing up the hospital hill to work on the new reservoir. The early morning is very comfortable and we try to get our active work done then. By noon it is hot, usually somewhere in the nineties. Most people rest or sleep at least an hour after lunch. About four o'clock in the afternoon it begins to get cooler and there is usually a nice breeze or rain. Darkness comes quickly about 6:30 and we finish our supper by electric light. The nights are quite comfortable; and morning finds us under a sheet or spread. The pace is definitely slower here than at home. We even walk more slowly. One great advantage of this climate is the fewer clothes that I have to get myself and Kenny in and out of. Kenny usually runs around in a pair of training pants and sneakers. Who cares if the pants get wet; he won't catch cold and the ground or cement isn't hurt!

You ask what we would like to have that isn't available here. First of all, seeds. We would like to try Swiss chard. Any summer flower seeds would be welcome: morning glories, nasturtiums, cosmos, petunias, hollyhocks, viny flowers. It would work best to enclose a few seeds in your letters. Books of every description are always welcome. Those for Kenny will be shared by the mission children and Sister Elfriede's African babies for whom they are a great treat. Sunsuits, too, are welcome. Wish you could come to see us in July to welcome a new grandchild.

YESTERDAY WAS Palm Sunday and the windows of the church were decorated with palm branches, which are easy to find around here. Our palms are quite a contrast to the hothouse variety found at home. In the late afternoon the Sunday school children had a parade through town. They were all dressed up in their African clothes (during the school week they wear simple shorts and shirts, or dresses). They marched along carrying palm branches interwoven with lots of bright flowers. They sang a song with *hosanna* in it and marched with great enjoyment. The middle school boys in white uniforms brought up the rear with a drum corps.

We took a ride to look for Easter lilies. Sure enough, there were some lovely blooms in a wet shady spot near the road. Dick found that the bulbs go very deep, and he had to cut them to get them out. Maybe the big plants will have more blooms by next Sunday so we can decorate the church with them. We have some cuttings of other flowering shrubs which we will transplant after they root in water.

We had a game night on Saturday and introduced the African and Korean games that Ted and Donna gave us. Now we can see why it takes the Africans almost a whole day to finish a game of Adi. The instruction book says the game usually ends by someone's giving up and going home. The missionaries here try to get together at least once a week for recreation, but it is hard to keep shop talk out of the conversation. At the moment there is another European family in Worawora whom we will invite. Mr. Williams, from England, is in charge of putting in the well and the pumps for the town. On Tuesday evenings we have prayer meetings. Dick and I would be in favor of having them on Wednesday evenings. Then we would remember our anti-malarial schedule. Our missionary formula for a healthy life here is "Prayer and Daraprim!"[2]

Dr. Whitcomb left on Thursday after spending nine days operating every morning. In the evening he and Dick would pore over the surgical supply catalogue hunting for equipment for Adidome. The request for an estimate of supplies went off to one firm this morning. It will probably be a little over $3,000.

You have probably been wondering what our helpers are like and how we are adjusting to this totally new experience of having servants in the house. All three of them are young, about seventeen or eighteen, and are quite small in size compared to American teenagers. Nellie, who does most of the baby-sitting, has finished middle school. Since this is equivalent to junior high school, she would be eligible to teach in primary school. She wants to enter nurses' training here, but I am urging her to find out about the fully-accredited schools so that she will have something more than just experience to show for her work. If she could pass the entrance exams, she could probably manage to pay the fees. She can save some money from her monthly salary, and her father, who is a cocoa farmer, ought to be able to help out some. Although she would be a dependable worker at either the Worawora or Adidome hospital, the real need is for qualified nurses to do a professional job.

Our houseboy, Tawia, finished the third term in middle school and could graduate in one or two more years. I hope

---

[2] *Daraprim* is the name of a drug taken to prevent malaria.

he can for he seems to be bright and should be able to handle more technical work than being general flunky in some European's house. He can coax our temperamental refrigerator to get cold and fix the plumbing in the Accra resthouse, so he is a handy person to have around. His name, Tawia, is one given to a person born after twins. There are three sets of twins in his family. His mother, one of four wives, had eight children; and the entire household numbers thirty.

The gardener, Kumla, prefers to be called by his Christian name, John. His Ewe name is that given to all boys born on Tuesday, so he and Kenny have the same name. Dan Schler considered him a smart boy and put him in charge of the Schler chickens and rabbits while Dan is away. He works for us part time, but we're not sure what part of the time it is.

All three of our helpers like Kenny, and of course he likes them too. We frequently find them looking at his books when they aren't busy. Nellie has picked up some of our nursery rhymes which she sings to distract and amuse her small charge. They are all Ewe speakers and can be of great help to us as we study. Yesterday we encouraged the two boys to go to church with us. We were dismayed when we failed to see either one present. On coming out of church we found them sitting on the steps of a neighboring house and thought they had been asleep. It turned out that they had gone to the children's service. Since the entire church service is in Twi, with an occasional comment in English, they probably got more out of the children's service with its simpler story than they would have out of the adult service. We are wondering how to make our family devotions in the morning more meaningful to them. We have an Ewe Bible which they read, but I am afraid the rest of the meditation from the lenten devotional booklet is totally out of their experience and beyond the range of their English. They give us a great incentive to learn Ewe. If you have any good devotional books for youth, send them on.

✦ ✦ ✦

Worawora, Ghana
April 24, 1957

WE HOPE YOU ALL had a very happy Easter and are now getting some spring finally to help celebrate it. I can't say that it feels exactly springlike around here, but we do have plenty of wild Easter lilies. Easter here certainly was an interesting experience, more so than Christmas in England. We were awakened before dawn on Easter by the Worawora "Easter Parade" composed of church women marching through town with drums and bugles, lustily singing "alleluia." We could hear them singing for an hour before daybreak (some of them slept through the sermon at church too!). The morning service was a moving experience. These people love to sing, dance, and march—and they do all these well. The children march through town on the slightest provocation. They even had a parade on Palm Sunday and again on Easter morning.

Church here is quite an experience. Actually we find it more worshipful than the London Anglican churches, even though we can't understand the words. The service is quite dignified except that spontaneous singing crops up occasionally, sometimes even in the middle of a sermon. The Worawora church is the head church in this district. It has a fully qualified pastor who spends about half the Sundays in outlying churches. When he is away, an evangelist or catechist preaches here. Pastor Forson of Worawora could hold his own with most U.S.

preachers. He always starts each sermon with a five-minute English abstract that makes an excellent sermonette. We are asked to sit in front with the church elders; the women all sit on the left, and the men on the right. In back are the school children in their freshly-laundered white suits. They parade into church singing. The choir is striking in its black robes (and bare feet). We enjoy the singing most, as do they. On special occasions like Easter, the Bible class (all members dressed alike) sings a special song. The children have their song—they sang "I gotta robe, you gotta robe, all God's children gotta robe" in Twi. Then the "Singing Band" sang the real African music that we really go for. We're getting ideas for the tape recorder. Sunday even the chief was in church. We have once-a-year Christians too!

The Good Friday service had a larger attendance than Easter. Because it was communion, the church was packed with four hundred persons. They don't hurry with the service here (I guess the women don't worry about roasts burning), and this one lasted three hours. It was altar communion, with a common cup, so this was one time we had no objection to their putting us first. It was interesting, watching all the rest of the congregation come up six by six—men in beautiful kente cloth or European dress, women with babies on their backs, the maimed and crippled. This was followed by special communion in the back for lepers, who had to bring their own cups. It is in times like these when we feel very close to home and to the world-wide fellowship of the church.

Ned Moser had to stay home from church on Friday to watch an obstetrical patient about whom we were worried. Finally in the afternoon we decided she needed a section but we were afraid to risk it. So Dick drove her to the government hospital in Hohoe, forty miles away. But the doctor wasn't there, so he had to take her another sixty miles to Ho where a young African doctor (with no more experience than we) did a good job and saved both mother and child. It is frustrating to have one of the best-equipped operating rooms in Ghana and yet be forced to send emergency surgical patients to the government hospital. At Hohoe they would have done the operation by kerosene lamp! We're just going to have to summon up some courage and tackle a few of these cases ourselves.

We had house guests over the weekend again. This place is fast becoming a hotel. The government tuberculosis specialist from Accra, a German named Koch, came for the tuberculosis clinic on Saturday and brought along his wife and nine-year-old son. We expected them to stay till Monday, but apparently they were bored stiff because they left before church on Sunday. Mrs. Koch hates Accra and doesn't see how we can like it here. They had never tasted any African food until we forced it on them. Though we tried, we couldn't persuade them to go to an African church. We felt sorry for them but I suppose that we should simply be thankful that we are adaptable.

Monday we went to the Worawora church picnic, which was held in conjunction with another church in a neighboring town. That was the first time we had ever gone to a church picnic on Easter Monday, but otherwise we found it much like other church picnics. There was a service with plenty of good singing and lots of speeches by pastors, elders, and even a chief. This was followed by plenty of eating. We brought our own food and it appeared as if our eating was the main attraction, especially Trudy's birthday cake (which did not last long). We were given some African rice and palm oil soup that was especially prepared for us so that it would not be too hot. It tasted good—that is the first few bites. Then we found ourselves turning all shades of red, breaking out in a hot sweat, and reaching for gallons of lemonade. Whew! We had never tasted anything so hot. At least it should have been safe to eat. We wonder if that soup is the reason why we treat so much gastritis.

In the afternoon they played games, especially musical chairs, just like the kids at home except that the music was furnished by drums and the players couldn't help dancing around the circle. There was drum music all during the picnic and always group dancing. Even Kenny caught the spirit of it and started twirling around clapping his hands—to the delight of everyone. The African children are thrilled to have a little white boy to play with. They can't resist touching his skin and hair to see what they are like.

In the evening Sister Elfriede (she's a German deaconess) had the Mosers, Mabel, and our family come to her bungalow for dinner. Having good German cooking was a real treat. Trudy especially appreciated it, for it was her birthday. That cake that Dick baked tasted as good as it looked, and there wasn't even enough left for supper. We've been having some trouble with our dried milk (Klim) souring, but then Trudy discovered that she can make cottage cheese out of it and so now we're souring it on purpose.

We have our breakfast devotions with our African helpers, but we don't have anything simple enough for their English. Might some of the children's family worship booklets be suitable? If you find anything, we'd appreciate your sending it.

Thanks for the lettuce seed. It's been planted by now. Our

first garden planting did not come up. We're beginning to suspect that our gardenboy is not very diligent, so we're standing over him this time. We could use even more seed—lettuce or squash.

↙ ↙ ↙

I GUESS THIS PLACE is even more like home than we suspected. There was a typical Sunday-after-Easter slump in church attendance this morning, and the preacher even preached about it: "Where are those who last week shouted, 'Hosanna'?"

The high spot of this last week was our attendance at a native (pagan) funeral on Wednesday. It had been going on for a solid week, but it took us that long to get up nerve to go. Since the pastor suggested to his congregation that Christians will not attend, we had to obtain assurance from him that our presence would not cause a bad impression. This was a big funeral for the local chief who died six years ago. They hadn't been able to get together all the money and other essentials to do it up right before this. And funerals here *do* cost money, for they are a big celebration with people invited from far and wide to make merry!

We can always tell when there's a funeral in town, for the most distinctive part of the celebration is a resounding premonition of the Last Judgment itself. Every few minutes, day and night for as long as the funeral lasts, there is a volley of gunfire. Anyone who has a gun is welcome, so people come for miles around with ancient six-foot muzzle-loading muskets. While they are here, they are furnished free powder to make a little noise. When we were present, there were about fifty guns going off singly and occasionally together. Our ears will never be the same. The drums go continuously, day and night, and someone is always dancing. Often a whole line of men and women can be seen dancing around a large fetish tree in the center of town. The dancing seemed to be directed by a few fetish women in nothing but loin cloths.

On one side of the proceedings sat the present chief together with the chiefs of nearby towns. They were drinking their share of palm wine (a reported fourteen barrels was needed for this funeral). On another side stood the former chief's bed all decorated with his pictures on it. In front of that sat all his relatives and official mourners together with his widow (referred to as Queen Mother!). His teenage daughters had to sit for hours motionless, dressed in nothing but ashes. They were very friendly (palm wine helped) and did not seem to mind our being there. In fact, they acted as though they were honored. A police constable escorted us around to pay our respects to all the chiefs and widows. They were eager to have their pictures taken. I hope some of the shots turn out well.

The big event of this last day of the funeral was to be a mock battle to determine who was to be the dead chief's successor. When we arrived, his stool was sitting in front of the other chiefs. We were told to watch it, for someone would try to get it. Just as we were beginning to wonder when something would happen, a large group of men rushed up next to us and fired off their guns all at once. When we dared open our eyes and uncover our ears, the stool was gone—and it was all over.

We were a bit disgusted by the whole thing. But when we

started thinking about it, we couldn't see that it was really more pagan than some of our so-called Christian funerals at home. They both seem to concentrate on being pretentious: the amount of money spent serves as an indication of a man's prestige. The money spent on palm wine and gun powder doesn't go up in smoke any more than the numerous flowers and expensive caskets. Actually, there may be more to be said for this custom. They don't insist here on having the corpse lie around, at least not after six years! Maybe there is value in having a funeral six years later, after there has been time to miss a man for awhile and to view him in proper perspective. And—does coming together to honor a person with singing and dancing pay any less tribute to him than walking around with long faces in pious mourning?

There's nothing pious about Kenny these days. Impish would be a better description. Trudy was preparing for the class of assistant nurses that she teaches, while trying to supervise Kenny in one of the big tubs. Suddenly Kenny was out of the tub and a spitting kitten was scrambling away after having had its first impromptu bath. Before he escaped completely, Kenny caught him and threw him back in. By that time the poor kitten had had enough and ran for the safety of the wired storeroom with Kenny in hot pursuit. Rackety made it through the screening, but his tail didn't. Kenny started to pull that when Mother came to the rescue. Rackety now avoids all water like the plague.

Recently Dr. Whitcomb reported that Kenny was putting things in the toilet bowl. That very day we heard a cry of distress and found he had thrown himself in, feet first. There he was, wedged securely, in the pose of that famous cartoon, "Good-by, cruel world." We find it awfully hard to be properly stern with him in moments like this. We put in our order for a placid second baby. But with a big brother like Kenny, it is doubtful that he would stay that way.

✒   ✒   ✒

W<small>E HEAR IT IS</small> spring where you are. You almost make us homesick with your accounts of tulips and redbud and a trip to the Ozarks. I guess we shouldn't complain. We too have lots of showers; and everything is green. It rains every day for an hour or so, but the rest of the time it is bright and sometimes hot. Even so, the nights continue to be one-blanket nights. The average daily temperature fluctuation is from 73 degrees to 93 degrees.

We finally have some beans, corn, and native peanuts coming up in the garden. Our second planting of carrots, cucumbers, cauliflower, cabbage, turnips, and eggplants was not any more successful than the first. Now we are clearing a shaded patch in the forest for the lettuce and starting everything else in boxes under the house. We found lots of cuttings of pineapple and papaya coming along well. The Doerings will reap all the benefits of these. We would like Swiss chard seeds sometime for variety. Variety is the hardest thing to get in our diet here. The native yams are good once in a while, but as a steady diet they constitute rather heavy fare. We may even stoop to requesting Kool-aid eventually. We use up about four dozen limes a week (about a dime's worth), but even that may get tiring.

We've been having fun with the African board game you

sent to us from America. Everyone around here likes it. One time we heard the plunk, plunk of marbles going around the board and caught our African helpers playing when they were supposedly cleaning the living room. They all know the game and the patients in the tuberculosis ward often play it. It's a popular game at big family affairs, especially funerals.

We are gradually getting more involved in hospital work. We both spend most of the mornings in the hospital. Dick spends his time in the clinic while Trudy supervises the tuberculosis ward and then teaches a nursing arts class every day. Teaching these people is certainly different from teaching nurses at home. It is difficult to teach a person to take pulse when he does not know how to read a watch. And it is not easy to teach him how to make a bed when he has never slept on a bed.

Attempts at the English language here are often maddening but sometimes amusing. The other day a night nurse's notes reported: "Patient had pain in stomach, but bicarbonate saved him." Trudy saw in the notebook of one, "When a person puts his wife in the hands of Christ, he gains strength to endure any hardship." Dick is finally resigning himself to the frequent clinic card complaint of growing lean for one day—meaning loss of appetite. Recently the hospital got a letter from a chief who had heard that we had a machine that could see through people, and he wanted to volunteer his wife to be seen through.

You just can't enforce Western ways on these people any faster than they want to accept them. At the moment Sister Elfriede, the German nurse and midwife, is upset over the way the patients are using the nice hospital gowns she had made for them. Most everyone simply wraps them around the waist, frequently ripping the sleeves. We have suggested that simple sheets of colored cloth would make just as satisfactory hospital gowns and would be more acceptable to the patients.

The hospital is also having growing pains in regard to the African staff. Some have been around long enough to feel they should have more status and not be just laborers, even though they have no formal training and thus have no qualifications as nurses. It is true, however, that some of them are now giving intravenous injections and anesthetics. They are now organizing a workers' committee and statements of policy are being drawn up. We hope they will soon have a sick leave policy.

The language study is coming along slowly. We can now hold brief conversations with our tutor; but when our patients talk so rapidly in their dialect, it sounds like a new language. Dick has now reached the stage in clinic where he can at least understand whether they are talking Ewe or Twi. Just one or two words in Ewe from him seem to warm up the patients considerably.

Dad, you will antagonize the Ghana postal officials if you persist in writing on the envelope "Ghana—formerly Gold Coast" or "formerly British Togoland." The St. Louis postal officials should be properly educated in the matter of Ghana independence by this time—so just write *Ghana*.

WE'RE IN THE MIDST OF the rainy season now and it is surprisingly cooler than it was last month. It still gets hot in the middle of the day, but it is not uncommon to need a light blanket at night. This valley is particularly lovely in the early morning when the mists on the green mountains begin to lift. This morning I am hoping the sun will break through soon because we have a big wash on the line. We'll have to stick to a regular schedule of sunning other things too, for we've discovered mold on our suitcases and shoes. Don't worry about the medical books, though. Dick's been giving them plenty of use this week.

Our garden does not benefit much from the rain. Nothing is there but groundnuts and cocoyam to benefit. Thanks for the seeds we received recently—lettuce, squash, and carrots. They will be started out in boxes.

This past week has been a very busy one in the hospital. Ned and Alice Moser were away in Accra shopping, so Dick and Dr. Whitcomb saw the patients in the clinic. There are always more patients here when Dr. Whitcomb comes—white hair adds to prestige. Last night Dick finished writing out the orders for the Adidome hospital. They totaled about $2,500. With the $75.00 gift from the Affton Community Vacation Bible School, we will be able to buy a stainless steel collapsible wheel chair. This will probably pay for the shipping costs also. We are hoping the duty on all this equipment will not be too high.

While Dick was so busy at the hospital we cut our Ewe lessons to one every other day. But we realized quickly that this just won't do for learning the language. We seem to lose ground rather than make progress. It's a matter of discipline as much as brains, I'm sure. I seem to learn Ewe most easily from the Moser washerwoman, who is a good worker but who knows no English. I *have* to make her understand. By the way, *Ewe* is pronounced with *e's* like the first *e* in *every* and a consonant that is a cross between *w* and *v*. We don't have that sound in English, so it is rather hard to explain. It is very close to a *v* made with both lips instead of the upper teeth and lower lip.

No, we don't see any snakes, although we have plenty of yellow-tailed lizards, if that will help! And no, we don't do the cooking or feeding of our helpers. They pay an African woman to cook their food and eat major meals only twice a day—about 9:00 in the morning and about 7:30 in the evening when they finish their work. They like very little of our food, except cookies and oranges that are sweet. The thought of cold food, especially cold water and ice cream, makes them shiver. They say ice cubes burn their hands. The staple items in their diet are yams, cassava, and rice. These they eat with meat soup, or palm oil, or groundnut soup, which is very peppery (red peppers) and thick, like gravy. The starchy food is dipped into the soup with deft, quick fingers and popped into the mouth with less muss than we make using forks and spoons. I feel very extravagant when I compare our food costs with theirs that average about two pounds a month. Last week when I had a surplus of bananas, Tawia was the only one who would take some home to eat.

I completely forgot to mention Mother's Day. I forgot it was coming until the very day. But you do know how much you mean to us. This year I felt unusually qualified on

Mother's Day, with one toddler under my feet, one kicker in my tummy, and three teenagers who call me Ma.

Our tape recorder is coming in very handy now. We discovered one evening last week that the current from one of the two generators is not up to the 50 cycles required for fidelity with our recorder. Now we enjoy our tapes at a half tone lower pitch and a slightly slower speed. When we record our Ewe lessons, the playback is fine. Our problem in making tapes for you will be to find electricity where the interesting sounds are, or vice versa.

All the stocks of Prime Minister Nkrumah's autobiography were sold out in Accra within a week.

✔ ✔ ✔

Worawora, Ghana
May 26, 1957

THINGS ARE GETTING BACK to normal since Dr. Whitcomb returned to Adidome. We are hoping now to get some Ewe studied. However Dr. Koch, the tuberculosis specialist, will be here tomorrow so it will be a busy Monday. Dr. Whitcomb's reputation has continued to attract the patients. But this is balanced some by the discouraging effects of the regular rains which keep the patients away. Frequently it rains two or three times a day, but usually it clears up between times. Everything *except* our garden grows like mad, and clothes are hard to dry. We're making good use of our two pounds of activated silica jel as a dryer, but we find that the things we can't keep in tight containers mold quite rapidly.

Yesterday Ned and Dr. Whitcomb went to Ho for the Evangelical Presbyterian Church medical board meeting, taking with them the African church elder on the board from Wora-wora. Dick has been appointed acting superintendent for Adidome during Dr. Whitcomb's furlough. That means being business manager. Dick plans to spend next week in Adidome to get oriented and find out what will have to be ordered for the house. If Trudy feels like traveling she will go along.

Kenny now has a fancy new plaything, a rocking boat which we had the carpenter make (for $6.00) from plans that Dick drew from a catalogue from the States (where it costs $22.00). It is four feet long and two feet wide, with a rounded bottom that rocks easily. It holds up to four children or two adults. Our helpers like to curl up in it. Kenny loves to rock in it, either alone or with someone else. But even this has not broken him of his love for the rocking chair in the living room, in spite of the frequent flights over its back after rocking while standing up. He seems to be recapitulating the boyhood of his father, for he is constantly covered with black and blue marks, scratches, and bruises. We never know where he gets them, for he seldom cries. His vocabulary is growing fast, both in English and in Ewe. He is such a little mimic that it comes naturally. He has to mimic everything we do, even crossing his legs when he reads his magazine while we read ours. Last week we had corn on the cob and he tried to get the whole ear in his mouth. Then he saw us and in a flash caught on. Now he's an expert. Incidentally, this native corn is not bad.

Since you seem to have been so astute as to do some reading up on the subject of Ghana, we shall try to oblige with some answers that so far have eluded you. If the rainfall is 28 inches in Accra and 58 inches in Kumasi, it is probably about 75 inches here and 30 inches in Adidome (all within a few months there). Recently it has been quite cool. A quilt has felt good at night. The rain does bring out the insects, but the house is well screened. The "mosquito traps" (double screen doors) keep out most of the insects except the innumerable ants and cockroaches. We did finally see a snake but it was quite dead. We were at Mosers' a few evenings ago when Mabel left for the hospital. She was back in a few minutes, slightly breathless, with the announcement that she had killed a snake trying to get into our house. She said she was afraid that if she went for help, it would get away. So she grabbed a broom and dispatched it quite thoroughly. We could not identify it. It was small, about four feet long, having somewhat poorly developed fangs and probably belonging to the viper family.

We're getting more fresh fruit now, though we haven't been able to find limes recently. Oranges are plentiful and the grapefruit are coming in, also a few pineapples. There's a fetish rule against selling pineapples in the market, so they're hard to find.

We see an Accra newspaper fairly frequently and hear the Ghana Broadcasting Service news occasionally. There doesn't seem to be evidence that Nkrumah is having any difficulty keeping control. If anything, he's stronger than ever. They seem to be deferring to the Ashantis quite a bit to keep peace, and quite successfully. The younger, better-educated people are interested in politics. We have met a few politicians who make themselves obnoxious with their self-satisfaction. But most of them have an understandable pride and humility.

Yes, we get plenty of vitamins and minerals. Drugs are available if we need them. We're getting plenty of calcium from both skimmed and whole dried milk. We would like for you to send a puree attachment for our food chopper, so we can use some of the abundant peanuts (groundnuts) to make peanut butter.

We finally got a copy of *The Messenger* mailed in February. We find that things sent to England and forwarded from there reach us long before those items sent directly from the United States.

✒ ✒ ✒

Worawora, Ghana
June 3, 1957

JUNE IS BUSTING OUT all over! Here it seems like we've been having summer three months already. What's busting out all over here is mold. Apparently we have only now entered the *real* rainy season. Now we know what is meant by a tropical rainy season. We still have a few hours of bright sunshine every day or two, but most of the time there's a damp misty overcast. Every morning it takes three or four hours for the fog and mist to lift—just like London (only different!). Then once or twice a day it comes down in buckets for half an hour or so. Occasionally we have an all-day or all-night rain. Having to dash out to bring clothes in is getting to be a common experience.

The Ewe word for July is *siamlom,* which means literally "dry me, pick me up" because everything has to be put in the sun to dry and then rescued from the rain. Our shoes mold overnight; and everything has that musty smell. When Dick reached for a tie yesterday before church, he discovered that it had changed color. All his ties are now the same shade of green. We concluded, along with the old-timers here, that there is nothing one can do about it—except to learn to live with the mold. We do have our valuables in air-tight cans with silica jel.

May 30, Memorial Day, was a big holiday here. It's the first time we can remember ever going to church on Memorial Day. This year it was also Ascension Day, which in the church here is on an almost equal status with Christmas and Easter. Apparently this is due to its German origin. There was a good crowd in church and they had special singing again.

We've started taking Sunday afternoon walks around town, which is a much better way of seeing the place and getting to know the people than riding around as we usually do. Last Sunday we walked out in the country on the road past the hospital, toward the little village of Apesokubi. We passed a small dirty well that people from miles around have been using for their water, especially during the dry season. There was only a small amount of water in it, and that was very dirty. Sometimes the women carry large pans, like dishpans, but holding up to four gallons, on their heads for two or three miles. It will certainly be a boon when the government finishes the town water supply.

We saw also where they were making palm wine. They had chopped down some of the smaller bushy palm trees and had cut holes in the trunk, through which the sap was dripping into jars. It was fermenting well, but didn't smell particularly appetizing! Yesterday we walked through the village and down some of the back alleys. Everywhere we went we set people scurrying—some of the adults away from us, but all the children scurrying after us yelling *obroni, obroni (European,* or *white man*). Everyone seems to know who we are, and they all appeared to be quite happy to see us walking around their town. We wish we could talk more with them. But anyway, they responded to *good evening* in English. Most of the women were busy pounding fu fu as we went by.

Dick had an experience Friday which makes us realize how far we still have to go in training African nurses to do even their small jobs properly. In the clinic he saw a four-month-old child very sick with malaria and ordered an anti-malarial injection instead of the usual oral medication. The injection room boy gave instead of the clearly specified 2/3 cc. dose, 2/3 of an ampule—or 3 cc. Jean Nagel called us down from lunch an hour later when the child was almost dead. Only then was the error discovered. We injected all kinds of cardiac stimulants but they did no good. Since we have no oxygen facilities, we just had to stand there watching the child finally stop breathing and the heart sounds grow weaker. Finally, as Dick was starting to tell the boys to bring a cloth to wrap the body, she gave another gasp and started picking up. In half an hour she was crying lustily. You can't convince us that miracles don't happen or that prayers aren't answered.

We tried planting some lettuce in boxes under the house away from the sun and it came up nicely. But then the lizards, which share the house with us by the hundreds, ate off all the tops. So now we'll have to think of something else to do. For some inexplicable reason the eggplants which we planted are coming along famously—ugh!

THE BIRTHDAY PACKAGE arrived today; what fun it was to open it. Three excited children were here to help me celebrate. Janice and Danny Moser were even more enthralled than Kenny because they know what packages are. They were pleased about the new books. Books and toys get rugged use here, for Kenny always takes a book or toy along when he goes to play with the African children. Brightly colored books are a source of great joy to those little ones (and their nurses too) because they see so few of them.

The Gelhauses, who have been here a year working on hospital construction, will leave for the United States in July. We hope to buy most of their household equipment, such as brooms and pails. The mission-owned furniture they have will probably be put in our house. We hope the Swiss contractor will let us buy his baby basket and playpen.

Dick and Doc Whitcomb have to go to Accra to buy things for the new hospital. How happy Dick would be if he didn't have to look forward to business responsibility this year. He finds the treating of patients more interesting and rewarding. He says, "Medical school never prepared me for this."

Kenny misses his Daddy. Whenever we sit down at the table, whenever he hears the Volkswagen, whenever he wakes from his nap, it's always: "Daddy? Daddy? Daddy?" so hopefully.

We need Sunday school material. There is none available in the vernacular here. Can you recommend some that we could get?

Dr. Elmer Whitcomb (center) shows settling basins of Adidome hospital's filtration system to visiting group.

Teamwork by Doctor Braun as surgeon, his wife Gertrude as anesthetist, and African assistants

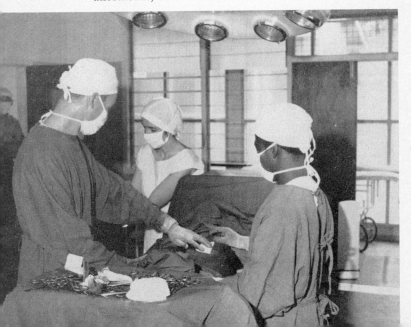

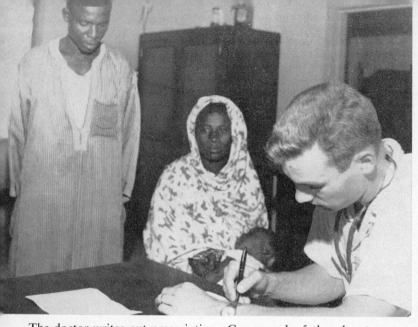

The doctor writes out prescription. Cap worn by father denotes Muslim religion.

This child may have bilharziasis, a common disease that affects the liver.

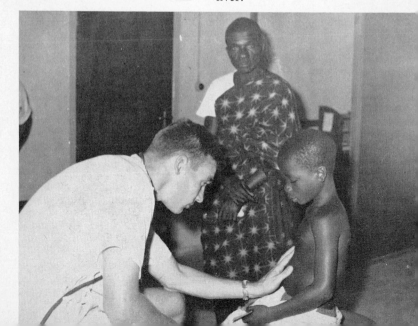

IT's GOOD to be back home and find that Trudy has not delivered in my absence, and that Kenny still knows me. He did
stare at me for a while before he finally said Daddy.

It was good to get home last night too, because for a while
we thought we would not get back at all. It's the rainy season
here and anything can happen. The road south of Adidome to
Accra is blocked by construction on a new concrete culvert.
The detour around it got bogged down in a marsh. Dr. Whitcomb had left his car on the other side of it. So when we went
to Accra, we took one car that far, walked across, and then
went on in the other car. The road north, forty-five miles to
Ho, was supposed to be all right (never more than a one-way
track) but it rained solidly all Monday night. There are no
other roads. About twenty miles out, we hit a place where a
small river had washed out the road for a few hundred feet,
leaving canyons two feet deep. We backtracked ten miles to a
village and picked up two men with shovels. By leveling off
the edges we finally managed to get across.

We thought our worries were over, though actually they
were just beginning. There were four more places where rivers
crossed the road. Each time we walked across and found the
road solid under the water; but each got deeper. I was amazed
that the car took even the first few, plowing through water
over a foot deep. But the last stretch was over a hundred
yards in which the water was up to my knees (twenty inches).
We could not turn back then and it was still raining. The
prospects were that it would get deeper rather than shallower.
So we tried it and plowed right in. Tawia stood in the middle

✦ 55

to show me where the road was. It's a strange experience to be driving with the waves breaking over the windshield. Then right in the middle we stalled and water rushed in the doors. We could hear it gurgling down the exhaust pipe. But to our amazement, the starter worked and the motor started. We pulled right through the remaining fifty yards. We must lead a charmed life.

After a few minutes of racing the motor to dry it off, we went merrily on our way—at least for three miles. Then we stopped dead as could be—out of gas! I knew we were a little low, but apparently these demands beyond the call of duty really burned up the petrol. Tawia started walking to Ho, fourteen miles away. We waited. Mabel Burket was along and so was an African girl and her seven-month-old baby. A lorry came by going in the opposite direction, but it burned diesel oil. However its driver was back in a little while; he could not believe that we had been through all that water that he saw. He gave me a ride to Ho. Dave Desmond of Mawuli school drove back out and we added gas, but it still took cleaning out the distributor and the carburetor before it would start. So it took us six hours to go those forty-two miles. But I will give a willing testimonial for this ranch wagon—it's fantastic.

Adidome Hospital is making rapid progress and looks great. The three wards will be ready for occupation within a week; but the other buildings and water plant will take longer. Our house is scheduled to be completed by July 31, so we should be able to move in by August. Our house will be pink and green outside. It will combine imaginative use of color and modern design. Tawia and I planted flowers, bananas, pineapple, shrubs, and a whole row of bougainvillia. But because the grass grows so fast, the mowers may cut them all down before we get there. We sure could use a full-time farmer down here to develop the 200 acres of good soil with its possibilities of cheap irrigation (that sounds ludicrous at the moment). Water will be pumped from the river at the edge of the property to our waterworks for sedimentation, filtration, and chlorination. It will then be pumped to our water tower for distribution. There will also be a tank for untreated water, with separate distribution pipes for irrigation.

The present hospital at Adidome continues to do amazingly well with all its primitive facilities. Dr. Whitcomb is doing a lot of surgery in his mud hut, about one hernia a day. I assisted on one and did two myself. There is a fine spirit among the hospital workers here. They are treated as partners. Accordingly, they work better than at other hospitals. And we need fewer employees! The fine spirit is largely due to the Whitcombs and Sister Dorothy Williams. It's an interesting combination of people we have there—a German woman doctor who is strangely independent, an English fundamentalist nurse; and easy-going Whitcomb. We are glad we are going there.

We all went to Accra for three days last week. Doc and I were busy looking over more equipment, checking with local steam boiler owners, and making the rounds of drug houses. We did get in a few good swims. Every time we go to Accra changes are evident, especially more new things in the stores. Here are some suggestions when you send packages:

1. All clothes are dutiable, whether new or old. Don't value too high.
2. All food except confections are duty free.
3. There is high duty on all toys, but books are duty free.

4. Don't put dutiable and duty-free articles in the same package. Duty is charged on postage of entire packages and on total evaluation.
5. Seeds can be put into first-class envelopes, but are often held up by the Department of Agriculture when declared in packages.
6. Packages should be addressed to a specific person, even if intended for the hospital.
7. Most items for household use are duty free.

✦ ✦ ✦

Worawora, Ghana
June 19, 1957

IT SOUNDS as if you are in the midst of a rainy season too. It takes a full force of laborers here working full time to keep the grass cut down around the hospital grounds. It's back-breaking labor as they hack away with their cutlasses. A power mower would be a great thing here; but first there would have to be a lot of rolling and smoothing and picking up of stones before it could be used. Corn that was planted a couple of months ago is now getting nicely ripe. Every once in a while we have a few ears to eat. Even though it is field corn, it tastes quite good when young and tender.

We have a new attraction at the hospital now—a white lady who rests very gracefully in the bed that we keep in our classroom. She came two weeks ago and ever since she has had her full quota of visitors. Her name is Comfort Akua, and she is a very nice model for teaching nursing techniques. Dolores Harkins heard that UNICEF would give these "dolls" to needy schools of nursing and so she applied. That was about a year

58 ✦

ago. Since then no one thought much about it, since the school of nursing is not established yet. Then one afternoon six big boxes arrived in a lorry. After unpacking the boxes, the girls found one big model and four other excellent anatomical models as well. They will be a real boon in teaching. We think they are as fine as any used in the schools at home.

Comfort Akua (so called because we hope the pupils will learn to make their patients comfortable and because she was "born" on a Tuesday) causes no end of amazement among the Africans. The women will stand in the doorway and talk to her. They wondered if she could eat. We told them "only a very little fu fu." Her very lifelike hands have been shaken so many times that they need to be scrubbed already. Visitors to the hospital regularly come to stare at her. They probably think we put some kind of spell on her. The ward attendants are very eager to study anatomy so they can use the models. Our Ewe teacher, Mr. Adzasi, is studying anatomy on his own initiative. When I suggested that he might like to see the model of the trunk with all the organs showing, he came at 3:30 the next afternoon. His usual time is 5:00 or 5:30 on Saturday. I wished that I had reviewed anatomy before I took him to see it because he asked so many questions. When he could think of no more he said, "I am speechless."

On the last two Sunday evenings Trudy has had a group of the nurses (all girls) come to the house for discussion and a brief worship service. Two of the American nurses were quite perturbed about the "morals" of the girls, so we thought that a series of talks about Christian marriage and family life might be helpful in guiding the girls' thinking. Actually when you consider that these girls come from a cultural background that readily accepts premarital relations as desirable and places the greatest premium on a woman's being able to produce children, their morals are not shocking.

The first meeting was mostly a lecture on the female reproductive system. The girls' questions showed their great concern about the ability to have children. Last Sunday we had a discussion on the desirable qualities to look for in a husband. The word discussion is rather misleading because there isn't much spontaneous response. Actually, questions were thrown out to help guide their thinking. But though they appear very interested, they are too shy and reticent to say much in English. How I wish I had a command of Twi for a moment like this. Of course I need also an understanding of the attitudes and customs of the people.

Before and after the meetings, the girls enjoy our game of Adi. Because there is almost nothing for them to do in the evenings, they seem to appreciate the diversion offered here. If in these few meetings they become aware of the challenge and satisfaction of creating a Christian home, the objective of the meetings will be more than achieved.

What a little character this boy of ours is. It is hard to tell whether his arms and legs are clean because there are so many black and blue marks. He is a real toughie. When he cries we know he's really hurt. One or two tumbles seem to teach him nothing. He goes right back for more of his precarious acrobatics. He rocks that heavy boat with a vengeance. When we get to Adidome we'll have to have a jungle gym built for him because there aren't any chairs and stools there to practice on. He thinks all cats are Racketies and points them out in books with great glee. He's a confirmed bibliophile. His favorite book is our Ewe dictionary, which he studies with great intensity just when we need to use it.

We surely would like to be at the Uniting General Synod in Cleveland with you. We have a personal interest in the merger, and we've been waiting a long time for it to come off finally. We'll be thinking of you. Please write us all about it. And we'll be eagerly awaiting the copies of *Advance* and *The Messenger* with detailed reports.

Next week all of the E and R missionaries in Ghana will get together in Ho for the semi-annual mission meeting (all except Trudy and Sister Elfriede, the midwife here). The road seems a little too bumpy for Trudy right now. Besides, someone who knows the ropes here needs to stay at the hospital. It will be interesting to see what these meetings are like. From all reports we've heard, it's the hard benches that leave the most lasting impressions.

✗ ✗ ✗

Worawora, Ghana
June 28, 1957

ALL THIS WEEK we have been thinking, wondering, and praying about the Uniting Synod meeting in Cleveland. How we would have liked to be there! Now we are eagerly waiting for firsthand reports. We hope the small CC opposition buried the hatchet gracefully and joined in with a spirit of Christian cooperation.

Dr. Whitcomb has been here since Monday doing one or two operations every morning and seeing patients in the clinic. As usual, he and Dick have many details about the Adidome hospital to discuss. Dick is convinced it takes even more talk than money to build a hospital. Harley Gelhaus, minister from Iowa who has been here a year supervising the construction of the hospital and the laborers, will be leaving the first part of July. Then it will be the doctors who have to check to see that the carpenters build things according to specifications and that the grass cutters don't lean on their cutlasses instead of chopping grass.

On Wednesday of this week, two Danish doctors (a man and his wife) from the World Health Organization came here to make smears of the sputum of untreated tuberculosis patients. The sputum was refrigerated and will be flown to Copenhagen for culture, reaching there less than five days after having been taken here. This particular aspect of the WHO research is to discover if the causative organism from patients here reacts in the same way as germs from patients in Europe and America. It was very interesting to hear about some of the technical long range research that WHO is carrying out. We really look forward to the chance to talk to someone with new ideas and a different background. That's probably one of our occupational hazards here—the tendency to become awfully ingrown in our ideas and attitudes.

I'll bet you never encountered the situation we found ourselves in this week. We had so much lemon juice on hand that two bottles in the refrigerator fermented. We canned some of it with simple syrup for lemonade, but couldn't put up any more because we didn't have corks for the bottles. If Dick brings back another load of lemons from the Trost garden in Ho, we're going to try canning the juice using coke bottle caps and candle wax. Hope we get some more pineapple too. Last time we bought ten. Of these we used eight, canning three quarts of pieces and one of juice. Mmm, there's nothing to compare with really ripe fresh pineapple! We've been experimenting too with ice cream made with coconut milk. It has a mild flavor easily covered by milk-powder taste. Next time I'll use more coconut. At the price of one coconut for twopence, the experiment isn't costly.

It's ironic that you are having so much heat while we who are just a few degrees from the equator are quite comfortable. During the past week we actually got up one night about 4:00 a.m. and rummaged around for another blanket.

The rains have slackened some. In fact, we *need* rain. The water pump is broken again and we have to haul water from the old cistern. A typical rainstorm here is quite an experience. The first sign of rain coming is a slight clouding up, often in the form of a low cloud that can be seen across the valley to the south. Then we hear it coming. When it arrives here it sounds like a freight train coming across the valley. But still there is no sign of breeze or fresh air. Then suddenly the wind starts blowing furiously; and if we haven't already closed the windows, the house is a mess within a minute. Once we were too slow and a mirror was torn from the wall. Then the rain hits like a pile of bricks and the noise is enough to stop all useful occupation. That usually keeps up for about thirty minutes. Then suddenly it ceases, although sometimes it is followed by a long, slow rain. Occasionally we get three or four of those storms a day.

We expected Dr. Whitcomb at noon but he was delayed. After a patient came in bleeding heavily, needing a Caesarian section and unable to be moved, we began to look for him desperately. Finally we went ahead and did the operation, sweated through it, and saved the baby. Now maybe we'll have more confidence to go ahead when we have to.

Happy Independence Day. We did not have any luck declaring a national holiday for us so that we could all go to the beach. But we will celebrate by having a picnic with plenty of lemonade behind the Mosers' house. We have been hearing about floods in Webster Groves [Missouri]. Here at the moment we're in the midst of a drought. We haven't had any rain in two weeks and the pump is still broken. The time between our baths has been stretching out further and further. For a few days a government tank truck hauled water from the old cistern. But now that water is gone too. No one knows when the pump crew will get here, and no one seems to be doing anything about it. We still have a bathtub full of water that we hoarded. We'll have to use it carefully. Oh, for a mechanic!

The mission conference at Ho was fun from the standpoint of getting together with the others, if not for sitting all day on hard benches. It was the first time Chuck and Gaby Hein and their two children managed to get over from the French side.[3] It was good to see them. Apparently they are having a hard time making ends meet over there where things are either quite expensive or not available. We wish they could be nearer. Chuck displays very clear thinking in a meeting. This session was primarily a budget planning meeting. It made us realize how expensive this work is and how much it takes to maintain a missionary on the field. We are not allowed to vote in such meetings for two years.

---

[3] From Togo, where the Heins are the first missionaries of the Evangelical and Reformed Church to serve in that land.

Sunday we had to work hard when we got a dozen patients from a lorry accident. Most of them were not seriously injured —mostly cuts, bruises, and broken bones. But the bus driver was deeply comatose and obviously had severe head injuries with bleeding into the brain. Since we had nothing to lose and everything to gain, we decided to try a craniotomy to relieve the pressure. Dick's internship served him well. We struggled through it with apparent improvement. But he died twenty-four hours later. He probably would have died even with the best neuro-surgeon.

Now we have a fifteen-year-old boy in the hospital with rabies. That's a pitiful sight to see. He was bitten by a mad dog three months ago, but the father said he did not think it was bad. Now all we can do is sedate him until he dies and try to keep him from infecting someone else.

This seems to be a good season for citrus fruits. We can get oranges two for a penny in the market. Yesterday we picked six big grapefruit off a tree for three cents. Dick still hasn't reached the saturation point on fresh pineapple, so we have it in some form every meal. Yes, powdered milk tastes as good as fresh milk. It costs as much as fresh milk at home, but fresh milk is entirely unavailable here. Yes, soap is available. We use Surf for dishes, Lux for bath, and cheap Key for laundry.

One morning after devotions Nellie said to Dick, "My father wishes to greet you," and led us to the kitchen. I don't know how long they had been waiting there. We took them into the living room and passed pleasantries with two very nice looking men. When they had gone I asked Nellie how old her brother was. She looked embarrassed for a moment and then said, "He is not my brother; he is my younger father." This was really confusing for though we hear a lot about polygamy around here, we hadn't heard of any cases of polyandry. Then it dawned on me that she meant he was her father's younger brother. The Ewes have a different word for each relationship: father's older brother, younger brother, mother's sister, and so on. In many instances a boy will inherit from his mother's brother rather than from his father. The word *brother* may mean cousin or an even more distant relation. If we want to find out whether two boys are brothers, we must ask them whether they have the same father, then whether they have the same mother.

We hear the St. Louis Cards are in first place. Amazing! Almost makes me homesick.

Worawora, Ghana
July 7, 1957

THIS IS Kwame Worawora writing. I've been out on trek for the past nine months and I just arrived in town yesterday morning, Saturday, July 6, at 6:40 a.m. I thought I had better make my presence known to you. My name is really Nathan Andrew Braun; but since I arrived in Worawora on a Saturday, everyone calls me Kwame. My guide on trek was Sister Elfriede, the German midwife, since all the other children around here believe it is impossible to be on trek without Friede. My only load carrier was Mommy, but she did not carry the seven pounds, four ounces on her head.

As soon as I arrived I paid my respects to my chief, His Royal Highness Daddy-hene,[4] who had sat on his stool await-

---

[4] The term *hene* is a Twi suffix meaning *chief.*

ing me two hours and greeted me with a gift of new cloth, plain bleached kente. I returned the formality by pouring a libation upon the ground, to the god of the wet season. There have been some drums sounding down in the village today, but Daddy thinks they are probably announcing a funeral rather than me.

Saturday afternoon Daddy brought my big brother down to see me and Mommy. Kenny really did not impress me a bit. All he said was, "Baby?" And all he did was try to poke a finger in my tummy. This afternoon I got my first ride in a lorry. It's much smoother than being carried by a load carrier. This was only a short ride, up the hill from the hospital to the big house that will be my home for the next month. I think Kenny knows that I'm going to give him some stiff competition because he sticks pretty close to me and Mommy so that he won't miss any tricks.

My best trick is eating, or rather drinking. Daddy tells Mommy she did not give me enough to eat while we were on trek, so now I have to make up for it. I drink four ounces of sugar water every couple of hours, but that doesn't stay with me very long. I sure hope they start soon giving me something that will stick to the ribs.

They say I don't look at all like Kenny did when he arrived, and I'm glad of that. After all, I'm me and not him. I have a wide face with big blue eyes and lots of hair. I'm 19½ inches long and my arms are almost that long too, which is good for scratching knees.

Mommy tells me I'll be almost two years old before I see my grandpa and two grandmas. That's too bad because Kenny told me all the fun he had when Grandpa Braun came to see him at the hospital, and how the grandmas came soon after to gurgle and make eyes at him. But I'm getting lots of attention here, especially from the African mommies in the maternity ward who had never seen such a small *obroni* before.

Daddy says that Saturday was really a red letter day, for besides me he got three issues of *The Messenger* (two from April, one from May) brought by slow boat from New Orleans.

Daddy says he wishes he knew someone going to Accra so he could send you a cable to tell you about me. He says the telegrams between here and Accra often get botched up pretty terribly, and he does not want you to hear anything but the truth about me.

Well, I think it's time to eat again, and then maybe I'll take a long nap. Kenny's giving me a good example for both those skills. I hope you will write me soon.

✒   ✒   ✒

Worawora, Ghana
July 14, 1957

KWAME IS a week old now, and already shows unmistakable signs of being a true Braun: he wants to eat all the time, likes to stay up most of the night, and sleeps all day. We now realize the advantage of living in a big house. We can just wheel his crib into another part of the house out of earshot.

Kenny seems to be resigned at last to the competition. His first reaction was his usual interest in "ba-bie," but he quickly sensed that this was a special baby who threatened his little private domain. And he showed his resentment. A couple of times he was disturbed at night by Nathan's crying, so he started screaming bloody murder and would not be comforted. But that did not last long. Now he takes a fraternal interest in the baby and likes to push his crib all over the place. He goes through the whole anatomy lesson with the baby: says "nose," points to his own nose, then flattens Kwame's; says "eyes" and then almost gouges the baby's eyes out. It will be good when the baby can fight back.

We sometimes wonder about our African helpers' attitude toward us. They don't often show any emotion, except to express dislike of the candied grapefruit peel we offer them. At our morning devotions we usually sing an Ewe hymn, then have a Bible reading in English and in Ewe, and then prayer. Sometimes our helpers choose the Bible reading. They are given a day's notice, but we suspect they sometimes choose at random. At least we hope they do it at random, for the other day Tawia chose to read the first half of Job 7, which starts: "Has not man a hard service on earth, and are not his days like the days of a hireling? Like a slave who longs for the shadow, and like a hireling who looks for his wages, so I am allotted months of emptiness, and nights of misery are apportioned to me."

We hear Martha Schlinkmann will be arriving July 19. We are glad, for we surely can use some nurses. We now have the first trained African nurse here, a boy whom Dr. Doering sent three years ago for nurses' training at the Basel Mission Hospital in Agogo. He is in charge of the medical ward now and is relieving some of the girls for other duties.

They had to dismiss a couple of the attendants last week. One was caught stealing streptomycin; another was aroused with difficulty from a deep sleep while on ward duty. Some of the white folks say all Africans are worthless. Actually, we think most of them do very well. It does point to the fact that it is not easy to instill a sense of responsibility in people who have no background for it and who haven't had the years of training that we have had. I don't think that a fourteen- or fifteen-year-old junior high graduate at home would do any better. The situation will improve when they get the eight nurses required by the government to set up a school.

It looks as though we shall have a couple of surgeons here yet. We are forced to do things we would never choose to do. Last week a woman came in late one night with a ruptured uterus—a real surgical emergency. We operated in a hurry, although of course the baby was already dead. Neither of us had even seen one of these cases before but we managed to get the rupture sewn up. The uterus should have been removed but we knew we weren't capable of that under the circumstances. She must have lost two thirds of her blood and she was almost dead during surgery. But she lived and finally got out of shock in twenty-four hours. Now she's doing fine. We certainly wish we could get some kind of blood bank, but it will be hard to get people to give blood. Two nights ago we operated on a badly incarcerated hernia. The patient is getting along fine now. If we're forced to do enough of these things, we may get the necessary experience to do them right.

We're not so lucky in everything though, and children are usually our heart-breaking patients. Dick has had three little kids die this past week. They just don't respond to the medicine because of their weakened condition and malnutrition. Some of them don't even look very sick, but they die quite suddenly. We could fill a hundred beds just with undernourished children who are able to struggle along for a while but who just aren't strong enough to continue to fight a little in-

Yams provide much of the starch n the diet; these were harvested in garden of Rev. Walter Trost at Ho.

There is no baby sitter problem in Ghana; mothers carry their children everywhere.

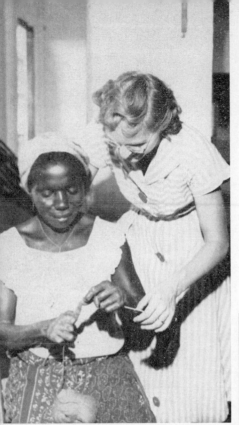

Mrs. David Desmond, missionary, teaching patient in leprosarium near Ho

The Braun family: Richard, Gertrude, Kenneth, Kwame, and Alan

fection or attack of malaria. These cases just don't respond to medicine.

The infant mortality rate is appalling, probably over three hundred for each one thousand live births. It is common to see women who have borne five or six children yet have only one or two living. Dick wishes he could devote all his time to pediatrics and child health program. Another discouragement is the obstetrics work. So often women come in only after they have been in labor for several days, or after native mid-wives have mistreated them brutally. They have some very potent native medicines, which when effective seem to relieve pain. But they often kill the baby or burn the mother horribly. It's going to take a long process of education. Some results are already evident. There are more normal deliveries and more women are coming to us who have lost a few babies but who want us to help them get a good baby.

We're wrestling with the high cost of medical care here too. At present rates a shot of penicillin costs eighty-four cents. That's a lot for someone earning $280 a year (the average income). This would be comparable to $12.00 a shot at home. In this slack season before cocoa is ripe and while money is still scarce, hospital attendance is lower. We have a feeling that people are staying away because they know they can't pay. We are trying to set up a rating system according to income. It's difficult because few people have a clear-cut salary or even know how much they make. And often they don't know how many people they support with that money!

Our Oak Leaf lettuce is thriving. After a month of cutting, it still is not tough or bitter. Eggplant is growing too—and (ugh) turnips.

WE HAD a nice vacation this week, though no one here was happy about it. All the lorry drivers in Ghana went on strike, protesting an increased third party insurance which we think is a good idea. A lot of innocent lorry passengers are injured in accidents. It's surprising how dependent this country is on its trucks. Everything has now come to a standstill. The market is half empty because most produce is brought in from other towns. Food is short in some villages, and almost no patients can come to the hospital. A few days ago we had only a dozen patients. Maternity cases continue to come in from Worawora. One of these was our second successful Caesarean. One obstetrics patient died while being carried the four miles from Apesokubi.

Tuesday we got an urgent phone call from a pastor in a village sixteen miles away asking that we send our lorry for a patient. On the way back the driver was held up by a group of union men who beat up the helper and stole the food brought by the patient. Someone remarked that this proves that these people are still barbaric; but just about that time the British Broadcasting Corporation reported a bus strike in the United Kingdom that involved the stopping of a school bus by a group of men who threatened the children. So I guess this proves that Ghanaians are now civilized. Such is "progress." However, they apparently have some valid complaints because they are requesting the government to bring back the English driver's license inspectors. The new African inspectors, they say, are too easily bribed and as a result unqualified drivers are given licenses. Well, we hear the lorries may be running tomorrow, in which case we will be swamped.

Kwame and Trudy got their first outing on Tuesday, when we all went over to Jasikan twelve miles away to "tea" with the government agent there. This was in honor of a new European family there who will be in charge of the district water development. The seven children had a grand time and Kenny remembered his best English manners for eating English biscuits and drinking Squash. The Thomases impressed us as being very fine people who have a genuine interest in the country and the people. They have a lovely bungalow on top of a high hill, with a beautiful view and nice gardens.

We have adequate indication of the value of religious education for the young. Kenny has finally conceded the necessity of grace before meals. A few days ago at lunchtime the food was not ready yet and Kenny was hungry. Trudy walked into the dining room to find that Kenny had climbed up on one of the big chairs at the table, had buried his face in his hands, and was repeating rather desperately, "Thank you, God" (Please, God, I've said thanks but where's the food?). He hears the African children call *obroni* (white man) when they see him, so the other day he looked at us and shouted *obroni*.

At three weeks Nathan weighs over nine pounds, so he is not starving even though he does not say grace before each of his eight meals a day. He sleeps better at night, but he still wants to stay awake eight hours a day and be where there is activity. I guess there just won't be any placid babies in this family. He was well-behaved in church this morning, however, and seemed to enjoy the singing. Trudy has tried nursing him during Ewe lessons, but her Western inhibitions prevent relaxation. So the baby gets no milk and she gets no Ewe.

The other day she put the baby into the bedroom to cry it out. Mr. Adzasi fidgeted for a while, then finally broke down and said, "Please go tend to your baby. I am not free." Africans just can't stand to hear a baby cry—usually a breast is immediately popped into his mouth. We had Mr. Adzasi to dinner on Friday, though he certainly was not "free" then either. He kept the table at arm's length and acted like we were giving him ptomaine. But he ate, and seemed to like the hot dogs. It was the first time he had eaten in a European home and had Western food; so it was a good experience for him.

The air mail *Messengers* arrived a week after they were mailed in St. Louis. We were so glad to get reports of the Uniting General Synod. We are glad Dr. Wagner will come to Ghana. We hope Dr. Hoskins can be persuaded to come too.

Our house in Adidome is now ready for occupancy, except locks on the doors. We are getting the furniture from the house vacated by the Gelhauses. We should be able to set up housekeeping immediately. Won't it be fun to start in a brand-new house—something we never dreamed of.

We are in the interval between rainy seasons now, but it has not let up much. It's been some warmer, but still not above 88 degrees in the past month. April to June is called the Little Rain, with the Big Rain from September to November. But this year the Little Rain has been very Big, and apparently it is going to merge right into the Big Rain. We're still getting corn, beans, and lettuce from our garden—and of course eggplant in profusion. Luckily Sister Elfriede likes that, so we don't have to waste any. Dick prepared a vitamin meal last week: boiled turnip greens, raw turnip salad, and such things. It was horrible! The squash from Stephanie's seeds are the size of baseballs now. They will taste good. The packages of cake mixes arrived safely. They look tempting.

ʟ ʟ ʟ

Worawora, Ghana
July 22, 1957

NATHAN IS GETTING big and fat, gaining almost a pound in two weeks. He seems like quite an intelligent young rascal—likes to lie awake enjoying the world, especially at 2:00 a.m. He follows us with his eyes quite expertly and prefers to sleep on his back. Kenny still won't do that. One of these days we'll have to give him a haircut. He'll probably acquire the African sense of rhythm at an early age. Nellie loves to hold him and rock him. She would do it all the time if we would let her. She passed the test that Jean Nagel gave Saturday. That was an exam for employment in the hospital as a nurse, so we'll be losing her in another month. Good girls for some reason are harder to find here than good boys. I guess it must be because there has been little impetus given to the education of women here.

A number of African workers in the hospital, mostly boys, have been coming up to pay their respects to Momma and the new baby. The prescribed formality in such a case is for them to say, *"Woe de le eme"* (You have come out from danger). Then Trudy replies, *"Yo, miawoe do gbe da"* (Yes, you have prayed for me). Trudy is fine now; she even insisted on playing flute duets this afternoon. But she still is not allowed to do any stair climbing. Kenny has had no more trouble with the new baby. He takes it all in stride now. His only regression is a diminishing of his voracious appetite and a sudden preference for a milk diet. He is making progress in his speech.

Ned and Jean Nagel were in Adidome this weekend to discuss hospital employee regulations, so Dick got a good workout. A boy died Friday night of internal injuries sustained in a lorry accident. We knew the police would require an autopsy and tried to get them to hurry up, but, as we expected, authorization did not arrive until this morning. So Dick has to miss church on Sunday to do the post-mortem. It was not a very pleasant task after thirty-six hours. He spent the rest of the morning trying to subdue a young acute (and violent) schizophrenic brought in last night. The family finally insisted on taking him home before we could talk the police into taking him into custody for transfer to a mental hospital.

Our hospital is half empty except for the tuberculosis ward. We hope business picks up when the cocoa season comes in and money is more plentiful. Sometimes we even have difficulty persuading very sick people to stay in the hospital. Last week an intelligent young man, who speaks good English and is now a college student, came in. He had broken his leg a few months ago but his father, an elder in the church, had not allowed him to come to the hospital and had insisted instead that he be treated by a native herbalist. The results were most unfortunate. We hope the Accra surgeon can still give him a good leg. Superstition still runs strong. Even one of the nurses, a secondary school graduate, reported in his night report that there were ghosts in the ward and that incense should be burned to dispel them.

It's interesting to hear that Stanley Wilke is planning an

African tour next year. By all means, come along, Mom Camp, and Mom and Dad Braun too. We will have plenty of room in our new house.

✗   ✗   ✗

Volta Vista "Mount Pleasant"
Adidome, Ghana
August 9, 1957

GREETINGS from cool, breezy Adidome, boasting sunny days and light-blanket nights in the month of August. Tonight we're wearing sweaters and have the doors and windows of our living room closed to keep warm. Wish you were here. We're looking forward to the time when you will come to see us in this lovely house on "Mount Pleasant."

What fun it is to live in a pink house! If you're feeling blue, all you have to do is go outside to see the rosy side of things. Dick came down here Thursday bringing most of our things in the Worawora hospital lorry. Between then and Monday, when the rest of the family came, he did a wonderful job arranging furniture and getting things settled. He even put vases of fresh flowers in every room except the bathroom. Since then we've had a happy whirl of days putting things in their place, planning where things should go, and talking to people who come wanting to work for us.

Until we send you a picture, a verbal one will have to do. The house is completely designed for comfort in the tropics. All living space is at second-story height, for the house is built on stilts. The rooms are arranged in a straight line and are entered from verandas on the south and north. The verandas and outside windows are completely screened. Since there is usually a breeze from the ocean twenty miles to the south, there will be air-conditioning all year round. All the windows are made with glass louvers that open and close like venetian blinds, so there is plenty of light whether we have the windows shut or wide open.

This is the ideal house for guests too. There is parking space for two cars under the house and seven generous rooms on the second level. The living room and dining room are large enough so that we can have mission conferences without crowding too much. It would also be fine for movies or square dancing since we have no rugs to roll back. The north and south walls are aqua and the end walls are light gray. This will form an attractive background for our wall map and Barosin pictures. The simple modern furniture that the mission furnishes has been upholstered in a cinnamon brown material by Mrs. Gelhaus and looks very good in the light room. Eventually we'll get a fiber rug for the living room and some easy chairs. The kitchen can hold two people with ease. The serving window to the dining room is a convenience that saves many steps. We won't be tempted to crowd into the kitchen to eat there. There is running water, a sink board, a small bottled gas stove, and a kerosene refrigerator that runs beautifully with a little coaxing. The light gray walls make the room look cool even with the bright sunshine streaming in through the west window.

Next door is a well-shelved storeroom (I did not say well-stocked: we need to go to Accra). The three bedrooms are blue, green, and green and terra cotta respectively—a lovely combination. There is a large bath that opens from the master bedroom and a toilet (with separate shower and wash basin) that is entered from the back veranda. The entrance to the pink study is from the front. It was fun choosing colors. The house is pleasant. On the ground floor there is a storage room and a room for the help. We are planting shrubs and a vegetable garden now.

If you are thinking that we live a luxurious life for "self-sacrificing" missionaries, you're right. The house, though a pleasure to live in, is more pretentious than we would have chosen. We fear it will present a barrier between us and the people we came to serve. It's easy for us to preach hygiene and cleanliness when we live in a screened cement house. It would be different if we lived in a mud house with dirt floors. We are hoping that when the hospital is moved over to the new buildings we can make our home a place where Africans come because they enjoy themselves and feel welcome rather than a place they visit because they are curious.

Kenny is finding the move from Worawora difficult to accept. He often asks for Janice and Danny Moser and Nellie and one of the garden boys named Musa. He follows us from room to room and plops down under our feet or climbs up and sticks his nose into everything. What energy! What curiosity!

I'm so thankful to have Tawia here to help us, for keeping up with two small boys is a job in itself. Nathan is growing so fast we can almost see a daily change. At one month he now weighs ten pounds, two ounces. He holds his head up quite well and stares at things. Yesterday he turned himself over from his stomach to his back. He has a tremendous appetite and insists on eating every two and a half or three hours. He eats cereal twice a day. Maybe we should try fu fu. It's filling (like cement).

Martha Schlinkmann is coming here to work with us. She's a fine person and her four years of experience in Honduras will be of real value here. There is a lot to be done before the opening and dedication of the hospital on September 8. The patients won't be able to move over for another two weeks. We're waiting for door handles and locks before moving equipment and records. Sister Dorothy Williams (the English nurse, therefore *Sister*) is getting the wards all scrubbed. We're waiting for the water system to be finished. They are having a hard time finding the right size gravel and sand for the slow sand filters. We have trouble getting the sedimentation tank to work right with the aluminum sulphate precipitant. Most systems are made for continuous operation but this one is for intermittent use up to 10,000 gallons a day. There are so many things we still have to figure out about running this place that we don't know where to begin.

✓   ✓   ✓

Adidome, Ghana
August 20, 1957

OUR PANTRY is now stocked and our house a little better equipped, so we're ready to receive guests anytime—whenever you come. While Dick was in Accra he managed to decrease our bank account $170 by buying food, bathroom fixtures, dining room linoleum, chicken wire, and two mattresses for the guest rooms. We are spending some of our gift money for these things. We certainly enjoy living in this big house. Sometimes we wonder if we will need to put in a furnace. The wind whistling around this house sounds at times like an Iowa blizzard. We're amending the name to Vindy Volta Vista. From our hill we can see miles around and across the river.

Our yard is beginning to look civilized. For a few days we

had four boys working on it as day laborers. We told them the best one would get the job of garden boy; so they worked pretty well. Now we are down to two boys who are busy waxing floors and furniture. Floors are of odum or African redwood; furniture, of mahogany. In our garden the lettuce and squash is already up. It's amazing what a little water can do to this land that looks so arid. Water is all any of this land needs. We have 200 acres just waiting for someone to develop.

One day Dr. Whitcomb showed Dick where all the surveyor's boundary markers are as they pushed around the three-mile circumference of our land through grass ten feet high. Dick was glad Elmer had his shotgun along, but they saw no snakes. We discovered that quite a few people are already farming on the land.

Right now Dr. Whitcomb and Dick do most all their "medical practice" in the new hospital. At 7:00 a.m. they make rounds. This consists of making sure the two contract carpenters are doing the work right, giving the two salaried carpenters enough to keep them busy all day, specifying how much gravel or how big a ditch has to be dug by the road workers, telling the two grass mowers what grass to cut, and keeping other assorted laborers busy. Frequently we have to "operate" with the picks, shovels, pipe wrenches, and hammers ourselves. We are finding that most of the workers have very little initiative and have to be told every little thing to do. We still have to check several times a day to see what they are doing.

The water system with three pumps, seven tanks with a mile of pipe between them, and two separate chemical additions (which have to be regulated by frequent laboratory analyses) is going to be a constant headache. We still have to find and train two men to run it. I am afraid running the system is going to cost more than we bargained for. In the meantime we have unadulterated river water in the taps, which works fine except that it doesn't quite get our clothes clean. We boil and filter our drinking water anyway. The light plant is ready but we won't use it for just us, so we get along with kerosene.

We were welcomed quite royally by Adidome. On the first Sunday we were introduced at church and given a few dozen eggs and two turkeys. Mrs. Whitcomb had a party for the purpose of introducing us to the hospital staff. This was a lot of fun; so was a "tea" for Trudy and the women's Bible class. The meetings of the women's Bible class on Sunday afternoons will be regular events on Trudy's agenda. They promise to be a source of real joy and inspiration. At these meetings there is first a Bible study read in Ewe by one of the three literate members of the group, then come questions about the lesson, then this is followed by singing. Often the women sing in the hospital wards or parade through the village singing. On Sunday each of the twenty-five women was introduced to Trudy by her Christian name. There are three Graces, four Comforts, and one Praise. Two women in the group are both mothers and grandmothers in families having five generations of women living in one compound. Several children attended the meeting, each sleeping peacefully on his mother's back. One of the women looked quite old to have two small children with her. They turned out to be her great-grandchildren whom she was suckling.

Rhoda, one of the church mothers (that's an elected office equivalent to deaconess), taught the group a new hymn. The members learned it by repeating the two verses over and over.

It's amazing how many hymns the women know by heart. Rhoda, though illiterate, is supposed to know almost every one of the four hundred hymns in the Ewe Hadzigbale (songbook). One thing that does not have to be learned is dancing. Wherever there is singing here, there seems to be an irrepressible urge to dance. Churches at home are just beginning to recognize that interpretive dancing can be a meaningful addition to worship. But here it is an established way of expressing joy in Christian fellowship. And the wonderfully graceful movements found here are thoroughly in keeping with these people. No straight-laced, long-faced Christians these! Can you imagine a women's Bible class in the States singing and dancing its way home after a meeting?

On Sunday afternoon we all attended a wedding party for one of the nurses and his wife. All the hospital staff was invited to the celebration that was held on Whitcomb's veranda. Clemence and his wife have been living together for three years and have one child, but did not have their marriage blessed by the church until last Sunday. He is the first of the nurses to have his marriage blessed. We're hoping that he will set a popular precedent. The ceremony took place in church after a sermon by the Rev. Walter Trost and just prior to a communion service attended by 110 people. Grace wore an African dress that she had made of beautiful white crushed velvet. Clemence wore a handsome cloth. We hope our color shots turn out well.

IT's LESS THAN a week and a half before D Day (Dedication
Day) and we're all busy trying to get things shipshape before
then. Dick was in Accra and arranged to have a lorry bring
back the 2,000-gallon diesel oil tank that the hospital is leasing
from Mobilgas. Now we can have our own ready supply of
fuel for the generator and steam boiler (if and when we get
that). The tank arrived and is now deposited in the big hole
dug by the contract laborers. Dick also got a new gas range
for us. The one we have been using was moved to Martha
Schlinkmann's apartment. Since our house will be the guest-
house for this station, we thought the nineteen pounds we had
to pay above that allowed by the mission would be well spent.
We are sure that we will often have to cook for many people.
We will put the new oven to the test when we bake cookies
to have on hand for morning brunch for the 120 officially invited guests on D Day.

The hospital is all ready to move now, except that the locks
have not yet arrived. Dick checked in Accra and found that
the ship on which the locks were cargo arrived in the harbor
last Friday. But since the locks had been loaded in the Neth-
erlands before the ship went to England for more cargo, it will
be some time before they are unloaded. We are going to provide seating for about five hundred people by laying planks on
cement blocks. After that many are seated, the rest will have
to stand under the shade of the palm thatch. The women of
the church are going to cook an African dinner of palmnut
soup and rice together with sweet cornmeal fritters. We are
providing cokes for drinks. Now we have to find plates and

spoons for the invited guests. We have already bought all the paper plates we could find in Accra, about fifty. In addition, each housekeeper here will lend her plates, including pie and cake pans.

The village chief and the paramount chiefs will be entertaining the chiefs of the surrounding territory. Our church members will furnish food for the people who are not on the afternoon guest list. They are going to buy half a cow to make soup for all those people. Incidentally, soup here means any kind of meat base food that is thick like a stew; and it's the main dish, not an appetizer.

The guest room here has been well initiated. Walter Trost was here Saturday night, the Duncans Sunday night. They are from the Scottish Mission station in the Northern Territories. They are doing evangelistic work in a new mission station six hundred miles from Accra. Before their new cement house was completed they lived in a mud hut in the village. They were thankful when they could move because the rainy season had started and the floor of the hut was one mud puddle. Living right with the people, they have made good progress in learning the language. Mrs. Duncan, a nurse, conducts a clinic every morning without interpreter. They are keeping in their home an African baby whose mother died. The Africans have no means of artificial feeding and cannot afford dried formula. They plan to return the baby to its father when it is weaned from the bottle. During this trip the baby was left with the father. They hope he cares for it well. They are able to make the 1,200-mile round trip to Accra only twice a year. They shop only once every three months. In their part of Ghana the people are much less advanced and still barter rather than use money to any extent.

The books you sent arrived. Kenny is pleased with his books about Betsey, the two-year-old, and listens very attentively to the stories about her at bedtime. Mom Camp, the *Reader's Digests* are put to good use here. After we're through with them, we pass them on to Tawia and the hospital patients. By the time they have made the rounds they are worn out. I sometimes wonder about Tawia though. The other day when he read the Bible in Ewe he skipped whole lines. If he does that in Ewe, we wonder what he does with English books.

↙ ↙ ↙

Adidome, Ghana
September 2, 1957

Great celebration here! We're sitting in our well-lighted living room listening to our recorder. Now it really feels like home. The recorder works fine with the new tubes.

But I guess the news you should know about is that Nathan was baptized yesterday. We suddenly realized that it was the last Sunday the Whitcombs would be here to be sponsors. Pastor Adiku conducted a very dignified service, though he was not accustomed to the English liturgy. Most of the other missionary children have been baptized by missionary ministers, but we thought it would be meaningful to the congregation to have their minister do it. So now he is officially Nathan Andrew Kwame Braun. We did not give him the Kwame, but apparently that's a *sine qua non* of local baptisms. We shall send some Kodachromes home with the Whitcombs.

To top it all off, the boom was lowered on Dick. Dr. Whitcomb said that as of today Dick is superintendent of Evangelical Presbyterian Church Hospital, Adidome. We have spent the entire day moving. Now that the outpatient department and the women's ward are moved, we hope to get the male ward transferred tomorrow. About twenty patients showed up this afternoon very insistent on being seen. They wouldn't go away even after we told them we were seeing only emergencies. So Dick finally had to rush through them, even though we could not give injections, do lab tests, or find a lot of drugs. The moving has been going remarkably well. The African staff is doing beautifully and things are rapidly getting organized. The locks and handles for the doors arrived Saturday, so things are still a mess as carpenters bore through doors and generally get in the way. At the same time we are trying desperately to get all the buildings and grounds cleared up before opening on Sunday. The places where the contractors mixed concrete or dumped rocks are still a mess. We started today to erect the timbers to support the palm-frond canopy for the seats and platform for the dedication. Even Dick is doing some carpentering; he's trying to build a speaker's stand from some packing boxes.

↗   ↗   ↗

Adidome, Ghana
September 3, 1957

WHEW! Where do the days go? If they keep up at this pace it will seem like just a few months till we go on furlough. Our fame must be spreading rapidly. On the first full day of clinic at the new hospital, over sixty patients turned up. Dick saw all the patients in addition to supervising the laborers and having a conference with Al Schwenke, accountant for the Evangelical Presbyterian Church. All day long there have been people streaming in and out of the house: four men putting locks on the doors, getting sawdust all over the newly-waxed floors, and putting safety boards on the stair rails; masons working on cement floors; people wanting to borrow things; and girls coming to see the baby. The whole place is a hive of activity. Martha Schlinkmann and an African untrained nurse have moved into the hospital, so now we have neighbors.

Kenny is hoping that some of our neighbors will be children. It's hard to play alone all the time. Last Thursday when we had supper with our African pastor, he was overjoyed to see the children and really hugged two of the little girls. One afternoon last week, four boys of school age came over to our veranda. They had great fun playing with Kenny's ball, and Kenny had great fun running after them. Before we knew it there were ten small boys all laughing and grinning at the antics of the little white boy. The children have school holiday during August and don't know what to do with themselves.

The pastor and his wife are very friendly to us. We enjoyed the meal with them very much. The food consisted of ground-nut soup, palm oil soup, rice, fried fish, and big patties of fermented cornmeal. There were also English biscuits and bananas for dessert, but the Africans usually do not have a sweet with the meal. We sat around a table and desk in the study, though as a rule African families do not eat together. The father and his sons will eat at the same time, when the food is ready. The mother and daughters eat later. (There would be a certain advantage to this if all the children were two-year-old boys!) Until lately the Africans did not eat for pleasure but just to fill their stomachs. It has been customary for them to eat only twice a day, once at midmorning and again at midafternoon. The next afternoon when the pastor, his wife, and some of their eight children came to pay us a visit and see our house, they were surprised to learn that all the canned goods in the storeroom would last us only a couple of months.

Nathan went on his first picnic last Sunday when we all went to eat supper on top of a big table rock about half a mile from our house. From the top of this solitary outcropping of rock, one can see for miles around. We could probably see the ocean with a good pair of field glasses on a clear day. Kenny had a grand time but we had to watch him carefully to see that in his jubilant dancing he did not get too close to the edge and slip down the steep face of the rock. As we were coming down, one of Dr. Windisch's enamel pans slipped out of our basket and bounced and clattered all the way down, chipping off enamel as it went down. Each of us watched it spin past but no one was quick enough to catch it. Doc wasn't able to find it in the thick undergrowth in the bottom. Oh, well, it wouldn't have been much use by that time anyway.

If our writing seems less frequent and less regular, it is because we are immersed in hospital duties. Trudy hopes to spend four hours a day at the hospital. Dick will be spending almost all of his waking hours on some kind of hospital work. He says to call him "Mr. Gildersleeve" since he's the water commissioner as well as superintendent. We were so busy that your letter was here two days before we had a chance to read it. We must get this off in the mail. If it misses the "collection," it has to wait two days for the next one.

THE BIG DAY of dedication has come and gone and we're busy getting settled in our new routine. I wonder if things will ever be completely routine. This morning Dick and Doc Whitcomb are doing a hydrocele operation, and yesterday they did an ovariectomy. Dick is really getting some experience in surgery before Dr. Whitcomb leaves. They are spending all their evenings going over financial books and trying to get details ironed out before the Whitcombs leave for Accra on Sunday. They will take the plane at 2:00 a.m. Tuesday and will arrive in New York on Wednesday morning. Fantastic, isn't it?

Last week hurtled by in one big effort to get everything ready for D Day. On Thursday the pipe bringing water from the river up to the filtration plant broke because the road under which it was laid had settled. The impact of cars driving over was too great. After some fast work and after driving the water installation foreman fourteen miles to Sogankope so that he could phone Accra for another pipe, we were finally able to resume pumping on Saturday afternoon. This allowed us to have running water on Sunday.

By Saturday evening we were all set. The palm-frond canopy for the audience was decorated with flags and paper streamers left over from the Independence celebration and donated by the district officer. The special speaker's stand was gay with bunting; and chairs and benches were arranged on the verandas for visiting dignitaries, hospital staff members, and guests. There were pictures and fresh flowers in the two wards, and new cloths for all the patients to wear.

The sound truck, recording equipment, and crews from

Ghana Radio arrived about nine o'clock Sunday morning. Soon after that our invited guests began to come in cars from Accra, Worawora, and even from the Basel Mission hospital in Agogo three hundred miles away. Many of the Europeans came to our house for brunch and freshening up. The Minister of Health and his "retinue" of officials arrived by river launch and were met at our landing by Dr. Whitcomb. After they had tea at Dorothy's they marched in procession to the out-patient department veranda. The ceremony began even before the scheduled time of eleven o'clock. We were hoping for bright sunshine to get good pictures. Everything was going along happily when suddenly just before noon the heavens opened and let go with a terrific downpour. The people under the palm canopy rushed for protection under the covered walkways behind the hospital. The chiefs under their huge umbrellas scurried to gather under the veranda roof—they didn't want to get their umbrellas wet! Thinking that the rain would be over in a few minutes, we rather welcomed this opportunity to get up and stretch our legs and visit with each other. But the rain didn't let up one bit. The people on the walkways huddled to one side and gathered their clothes up around their knees to keep them dry. After twenty minutes or so, the pastor tried to gather the people by starting a hymn. Then the speakers started to shout over the public address system. It's doubtful though that anyone but those directly in front of the speaker heard a thing. The rain made a terrific din as it pounded down on the corrugated roofs.

At 1:30 in the afternoon there seemed to be a slackening and Trudy dashed home to feed Nathan. Surprisingly the house was still standing in spite of the numerous kids running through and under it. The program finally finished about three o'clock and was followed by an official inspection of the hospital. Over 120 invited guests gathered for a cafeteria style luncheon at the laundry. Luckily the Adidome church women had taken in the huge pots of rice, soup, and meat stew from the small clay stoves outside. In addition to the African food, the missionaries furnished cokes, oranges, and bananas to complete the meal.

The rain ruined the outdoor decorations and mud got tracked all over the shining floors. But aside from these minor matters, the general spirit of the occasion was little dampened —except for the chiefs. They were miffed because a special place had not been designated for them to come in out of the rain. In the evening the staff gathered here for supper (we hadn't had time to eat much during the day). Now the real work of making this fine, modern institution into a means of Christian witness and healing begins. It will be no easy job. We will need equipment, personnel, patience, and prayers.

Josephine, the girl who worked for Mrs. Hazel, began working for us last Thursday. She's nice to have around and the children really enjoy being with her. Yesterday she put Nathan on her back. He liked this so much that he howled like mad when she put him down. We wish we knew how much he weighs. The food scales in the pharmacy weigh only to ten pounds and he's above that.

By THIS TIME the Whitcombs will have reached New York. On Friday evening of last week there was a hospital staff party to wish them "bon voyage." We played a number of games but the one that made the biggest hit was Bible charades. Each of four groups was assigned the dramatization of a different biblical incident, such as the crossing of the Red Sea or the battle of Jericho. The last one presented was the Good Samaritan, with Dorothy Williams coming in as the Samaritan's donkey. What a sight—thin little Dorothy on all fours with dish towels for ears and braided aprons for a tail!

We had a turkey dinner in honor of the Whitcombs on Saturday. The turkey was one of the pair given to us when we moved to Adidome. The meat was very good but, alas, after nine servings there were no leftovers except a few bones for soup. We didn't have pumpkin pie or mincemeat pie, but we did have baked squash and cranberry salad to go with the turkey. These cranberries are canned Scottish berries, much smaller than ours and purplish in color. The dessert was ice cream and confetti angel cake (Yes, Mom Braun, the one you mailed in March!). It looked beautiful with cherry frosting and tasted even better. Pastor Adiku and his wife were our guests for this typical American dinner. We could not tell whether they liked the food or not.

The Whitcombs bade farewell to Adidome on Sunday. After church many people shook hands with them and the women's Bible class came out here to sing and dance once more before Mrs. Whitcomb left. The women all wore their "dedication dresses" made out of pretty flowered material. After the car was out of sight on its way to Accra, the women came back into the house for a drink and a tour. The thing that impressed them most was not the kitchen or the bathroom, although they exclaimed over them, but Kenny lying in his crib. They had never seen a bed like that before nor a child of that age perfectly content to sleep by himself. (Ken didn't stay asleep very long with twenty-two mammas peering at him.) The pastor's wife had great fun demonstrating Kenny's rocking boat to some of her friends.

Both Kenny and I were overjoyed last week to find that one of the nurses has a little boy his age. We're hoping that Kwaku will come to the nurses' hostel very often to stay with his mother. He and Kenny are content to sit in the sandbox for an hour at a time making mud pies and enjoying each other's company even when they don't speak the same language. It won't be long before they understand each other quite well.

Dick and Martha went along to Accra to get hospital supplies. While there they saw "The Living Desert," a motion picture showing in town. But the most surprising American export they found was the American food products at the U. S. Food Fair. One of the big stores is now stocking Pillsbury cake mixes and Hormel tamales. Cake mixes cost fifty cents for the plain mix and seventy-five cents for angel cake mix.

In spite of the shortage of eggs, I have done more baking the past month than I did my first two years of married life. There's no supermarket here to buy baked goods. Just last week Dorothy brought me one hundred pounds of sugar and fifty pounds of flour. I hope these supplies will last four months. Eggs seem to be a bit more available here than in Worawora. We are the foster parents of the Whitcombs' four hens and rooster while they are away, so we hope to have a small supply of fresh eggs for Kenny and the baby. We had decided not to keep chickens ourselves because the chicken feed is very expensive and the feeding is just one more detail to keep track of. But if our experience with these chickens is satisfactory, we may change our minds.

Asiatic flu has arrived in Ghana. The number of reported cases is over 14,000, with eleven deaths so far. The district around Worawora reported over 70 per cent of the population down with it. Here several of the nurses have been off duty for three or four days and more people drag around not feeling well. Tawia was sent home with a fever of 102 degrees. Now that we all have been thoroughly exposed, we expect to come down with it any day. I just hope Kwame escapes; he's a bit young for flu.

D Day marked the beginning of the second rainy season and now we are having rains every day. Our garden looked nice until insects got into the beans and squash. Since we had no insecticide, we sprayed the plants with something like Flit and found to our bitter disappointment that it was not the best thing to do. The garden boy must have drenched the plants, for they turned black and expired. Perhaps the Whitcombs will bring us a garden book. We need it.

Mom Camp, the layette finally arrived. The box was sent to Worawora, then Ho, then Accra, then here. Half of the things were hanging out of the package but I don't think anything is missing. I am glad also to get the supply of thread and pins and needles.

I⟞'s Dick back at the keyboard again after a few weeks' absence. Can't say that I'm less busy now, but Trudy also is putting in an eight-hour day (including evenings) at the hospital. Things are beginning to settle down into something of a routine, although life certainly is not dull. The twenty-four wooden beds (no springs, no mattresses) from the old hospital are full constantly. At the moment about eight additional patients are on the floor. We will be glad when the new beds come, but we still haven't received word that they have been shipped.

Surgery is still going strong. I don't know if we are still living on Whitcomb's reputation or what, but they sure come flocking in. Monday I did a hernia on a young fellow, son of the richest man in Adidome, who quite willingly paid fourteen pounds ($40.00) for the privilege of moving his own bed into one of our private rooms. Last night he suddenly appeared on our veranda, after a quarter-mile walk, to report that he was feeling better!

These cases we can handle, but then we have been getting some that we have been forced to handle against our wishes. Friday night a hernia that had been incarcerated for five days came in. We ended up resecting the bowel most of the night. He gave us some anxious days, but now he is doing all right. Then at 2:00 a.m. last night a woman came in supposedly aborting, but this morning we finally woke up to the fact that she wasn't and so we spent the afternoon fixing up her ruptured ectopic pregnancy. These are things I would not have dreamed of doing even a month ago. But there is lots of good moral support around here, even if not much practical assistance.

We had an interesting patient Tuesday, probably the most powerful person in this district—the fetish priest from a nearby village. We are told that patients came to him from two hundred miles away and that he controlled his whole village with elaborate rituals and witchery. Naturally that village, where there are no Christians at all, became the chief objective of Sister Dorothy's evangelism. At first she was repulsed completely, almost thrown out. But just a few months ago she got permission to hold an open-air service there and she says she was received quite warmly. The old witch doctor finally told her that if he could only read, he might believe what she was saying. It was a concession for him to allow himself to be brought to the hospital, and quite a surprise for all of us. But he was extremely ill with acute liver degeneration (too much palm wine and crocodile bile), and he died the same day. Dorothy stayed with him most of the time. She is convinced that before he died he believed and was saved. Perhaps she is right.

Our biggest worry at the moment is water. We are afraid that there will be so much of it that we will be without it. The river has flooded higher and about a month earlier than usual. This morning it was within two inches of the top of our road to the river, which is built up six feet above the fields. Our pump house on the river bank is plenty high, but the pipe is in the road. We are afraid the backwater on both sides of the road will wash it away or undermine it and break the pipe. The river is still rising and this afternoon we had another heavy rain. I am having our pumpers keep the tanks as full as possible, in case something breaks. The water plant is functioning well now and we have nice clean water with a definite chlorine taste. I think we'll be able to stop boiling and filtering our water soon.

The lead news on all our recent broadcasts and in all Ghana papers is about Arkansas and the National Guard. It's going to take a long time for our country to live that publicity down. We keep our *Time* with Faubus on the cover well hid lest our kids see it. I believe Nkrumah must have been referring to this Tuesday when he made a speech justifying some of the government's recent totalitarian actions and warning against "hypocritical criticism" from abroad. People here are watching Americans just as much as Americans are watching Ghana.

Kwame has suddenly turned into the placid baby we had hoped for. He sleeps twelve hours in a stretch at night and is now on three meals a day, but he must have a banana at each meal! He stays awake for four or five hours in the afternoon, just gurgling and cooing as long as there is someone around to listen. Maybe the fact that Josephine carries him around on her back has something to do with it.

We've been enjoying the fruits and flowers of the Whitcomb garden. A stalk of pink bananas and a pawpaw ripened in our storeroom. They tasted very good. Snapdragons are blooming beautifully. We are now reluctantly enjoying one of the Whitcombs' chickens. Sonny, the Whitcomb garden boy, came and told me one of the hens was sick. Sure enough, it had diarrhea. I went through the prescribed treatment, permanganate in water and crushed clove of garlic, but the chicken looked worse hourly. The only thing I had not tried was cod liver oil. Since the dispensary was closed, I gave it a shot of Nathan's vitamin drops. Boy, the old hen perked up and started pecking with renewed vigor. However the improvement was only temporary and a short while later she drew her last breath. She did make a tasty groundnut soup.

This morning Dick assigned Victor, our mission driver, to haul some gravel to reinforce the road weakened by deep water on either side. As Victor backed the Chevy to dump the gravel, the car slid off the road and was left balancing precariously over the side with five feet of water just below. The laborers were not able to budge it, so with great misgivings Dick found a lorry and drove down to pull it out. Luckily it worked with no mishaps. From now on we'll haul gravel with wheelbarrows.

✒ ✒ ✒

Adidome, Ghana
October 7, 1957

WE'RE GLAD the Whitcombs are now in the States to give you a firsthand report and to answer all your questions—we can't keep up with them all. The black and white pictures we promised you are ruined. The water was too warm. And we learned that the Ghana Broadcasting System erased the tape of the hospital dedication ceremony by mistake before we had a chance to copy it. So that occasion is lost to posterity. Maybe we will have another noteworthy event. The Prime Minister is coming to inspect the hospital on October 27.

Well, Ole Man River, African style, has done took our road and pipe. We tried pumping last Thursday, but no luck. So evidently the pipe is broken somewhere under the four feet of water. The river has now crossed the road and swept away a section twenty feet wide and eight feet deep. The pipe extending over that space cannot stand too much strain. The river is no longer rising, though it seems to have no notion of going away. Luckily we managed to fill our tanks so that we had about 20,000 gallons on hand when the pumping stopped. We're rationing severely—water only one hour in the morning and one hour in the evening. That is needed mostly for flushing latrines. At this rate it should last us three weeks. By that time we hope the river will be down and the pipe fixed. If not, we shall start a bucket brigade. The high water has kept patients away. They are afraid to cross the river in their little canoes. Hospital attendance is very low and income barely enough to pay wages.

We thought about all of you yesterday as we participated in World-wide Communion Sunday about six hours ahead of you. We certainly don't feel any basic difference in having communion here than at home. The service is very much the same. Is it all-important that we cannot understand the words? The main difference to us is the atmosphere of the tin-roofed and open-sided church. We feel more at home here than we did in England.

We just heard about the earth satellite launched by Russia. I'll bet there's consternation in Washington! That's probably the most significant scientific event since the atom bomb. Incidentally, the Ghanaian press is really patriotic. The Accra newspaper reports that the traffic lights for Accra have been ordered in the special colors of the Ghana flag—red, green, and yellow!

The Asiatic flu has come and gone in a widespread epidemic all during September. Still it was not as serious as it might have been. None of the missionaries here got it, but most of our staff was down with it at one time or another. We still have a few pneumonias attributable to it, but on the whole it's gone. We find aspirin as good as anything for it, along with bed rest (which is impossible to enforce around here).

We still haven't heard how the world series came out in the States, or even who played. We presume it was New York and Milwaukee. Anyway we opened the season in Adidome last Saturday with batting practice. Some of the fellows take to it very rapidly. Maybe we'll have a good team soon. Many thanks for the gift of bats and balls. We split evenly with Worawora: we have two bats and a ball; Worawora has one bat and two balls!

You should see the suntan Dick has. Only the most prosperous MD's at home could afford to have one like this! Trudy has one too. And at night while we were giving Kenny his bath we scrubbed his ankles for minutes before we realized the brown won't come off. We finally got a baby scale and find that Kwame at three months weighs over 15 pounds. He's fat: must be bananas and Jersey milk he's getting. Ken weighs 27½ pounds and is 34 inches tall. They are both pretty healthy specimens and the source of much interest for all the Africans who see them.

We had a "bon voyage" party for Dorothy Saturday night. Outdoor games—baseball and badminton were planned for the afternoon. But only a few came. Almost everyone came at five o'clock for refreshments and talk. Five of the boys who are nurses got up and gave speeches of appreciation of what Dorothy has done for them. One of them even composed a song for her. This was very appropriate because that's just what she likes to do for special occasions. It had a good tune too. For us the best part of the whole shindig came when some of the fellows danced. What rhythm and movements. We have never seen anything like it at home. My, how we will miss

Dorothy—and count the months till she comes back in early June! Now Martha has the whole responsibility for the nursing staff with only part-time help from Trudy—a terrific job for one person. Can't you find us a hospital manager and another nurse?

It seemed like Christmas on Friday when a big shipment arrived from the United States. There were surgery instruments, operating room lights, tables, and beds from the Deaconess Hospital in St. Louis. We have the laborers working on landscaping now. Dick is gradually picking up bookkeeping skills. It's a great satisfaction to have books balance after a month. A trip to Accra was necessary to facilitate customs clearance. It takes weeks to do things by mail. We must have everything in order for the Prime Minister's visit here. I doubt whether we'll have a chance to discuss with him Ghana's political events. We read more about those in U. S. magazines than in the local press. The local papers are all filled with Little Rock events!

When last week we saw a picture of the paratroopers outside the Little Rock school, we knew that things had really broken loose. Although none of the Africans here has said anything about the affair to us, we know that this has had a very bad effect on the prestige of the United States, for there are almost daily reports about it in the papers and news reports on Ghana Broadcasting. That guy Faubus has done more damage than he ever imagined.

Chicken houses in Ghana, made of grass to insulate from intense heat of the sun

In a small village near Adidome mother and four children eagerly await arrival of hospital nurse.

Doctors Whitcomb and Braun check shipment of multi-purpose
food from Church World Service.

Pastor E. T. Adiku, of Adidome, conducts evangelistic service;
Dr. T. C. Braun, Richard's father, speaks for American visitors.

I⊤'s 8:30 Tuesday morning. If we get this letter to town in half an hour, the launch will take it to Ada. Otherwise it waits another two days before it leaves. Guess we should feel that our mail service is excellent. Martha tells us she got mail only once in ten days in Honduras.

The happiest event of the last week came when the water was turned on for unlimited use. The emergency forcing us to ration the use of water to two hours daily is now past. The river has not receded but our "fitter" Jonathan was able to move the pump up the road and start it at another spot where some of the overflow is several feet deep. What a joy to be able to take showers again! We don't know yet when we will be able to fix the pipe that is broken. We are told that the river should begin to go down on the 15th—and that's today.

The number of patients coming to the hospital during the flood of the last two weeks has been markedly lower than before. But except for lack of income, we have enjoyed the respite and the chance to get a little planning done. Martha and Trudy are planning to start a series of classes for the nurses and pharmacy boys as soon as possible. Their knowledge of hygiene and diseases is about comparable to that of an eighth-grader at home. The nurses seem interested and receptive to any informal teaching that we give them, so more systematic teaching should add to their interest and responsibility in their work. At the beginning of November we are going to institute the plan of charging patients according to their ability to pay. There has been a rumor around that we have to charge a lot to pay for the nice equipment we have.

Wednesday evening—the slight delay was caused by the sudden appearance of a drug salesman from Accra. He gave us a lot of free samples as usual, but it was our responsibility to see that he was wined and dined. Following that, Dick was forced into his first Caesarean section at the new hospital. The girl, who was very young, came through fine even though she had already been in labor thirty-six hours, but the baby was dead. At least now Dick knows he can do such an operation if he has to. But we hope next time the patient will be in good enough shape that he can give a spinal. We had a hydrocele operation today and will have a hernia tomorrow.

When both of us spend most of our time at the hospital, it is a great help to have Josephine and Tawia here at home with the children. Josephine is a fine Christian girl who comes from a town where there has been a Christian church and school for many years. She is more responsible and warmer in her relationships than most of the African girls we have met, and she seems to enjoy the children very much. Kenny calls her "Jose-me" and wants her to carry him on her back the way she does Kwame. Kwame responds to the warmth and security of being carried that way by promptly falling asleep. Josephine worked for Mrs. Hazel for two years and came to help us while Vivian is on furlough. She's a good cook and makes delicious bread and rolls. We have been introduced to a variety of African dishes by her. The food she prepares is quite tasty. She leaves out the pepper when she is cooking for us. Eventually Josephine wants to have her own business as a seamstress, with a stall in the market of her village. While working at Ho she saved enough money to buy a new hand-powered Singer sewing machine. She now earns extra money by sewing for others and for the hospital. She is going to make Trudy a dress —without the use of a pattern!

We have had daily rains and the garden is growing well. It is hard to believe it is October; it feels like June. How about sending us a package filled with the scent of burning leaves and a harvest moon and the taste of hot dogs at a football game. Enough of this nostalgia. At least we don't have to get out winter clothes or buy fuel for the furnace or bid farewell to fresh tomatoes for a season.

✦ ✦ ✦

Adidome, Ghana
October 28, 1957

THIS PAST WEEK has been a busy one and about as exhausting as could be even though the outpatient load remained light— only twenty a day. The high river and dangerous travel accounts for the lighter load. Last Sunday we packed off for Accra to speed delivery of shipments of equipment that had just arrived. There were seven cases of second-hand operating chairs, operating room lights, and a dressing cart from the Deaconess Hospital in St. Louis—all sent by Church World Service. Many of the things were the very ones that Dick had to clean often while working as operating room orderly there almost ten years ago. The lights are in good condition. If we can convert them to 230-volt power without too much difficulty, they should be quite serviceable.

The beds, 830 cubic feet of them, caused us trouble. Dick spent a complete day and a half getting them cleared through customs. The process involved all kinds of hurdles. At first the customs officials wanted to charge duty on the mattresses (we had had only a verbal assurance from the customs comptroller that they would be free). We finally got out of that. Then we were told that our import license was completely invalid because the request had been made for only twenty beds and we had thirty. To make matters worse, someone had written in the new figure over the government stamp. So we had to go through the whole procedure of obtaining a completely new import permit, which normally takes two weeks. Finally on Tuesday afternoon just before closing time we managed to get the three lorries loaded and on their way. By that time the stuff had lain around the customs wharf so long that we had to pay an extra $55.00 storage charge.

In the meantime Trudy managed to restock our larder and do some hospital buying. We got in a little pleasure—a good swim. We managed also a dinner out and a movie. Kenny likes the ocean so much that he almost drowned in it. We saw two interesting movies about outlaws. Walt Disney's "The Littlest Outlaw" was very enjoyable. The other, a newsreel of the Little Rock outlaw, really made us sink down in our seats and want to go and hide.

We got back Wednesday night and spent Thursday madly unpacking the whole raft of crates and all $8,000 worth of equipment. By nightfall all the beds were up in the wards and all the new instruments on the shelves. The reason for our haste was not to prepare for Kenny's birthday the next day. That occasion was almost eclipsed by the visit of the Great Man. Kwame Nkrumah opened a new government building at Sogankope, fourteen miles from here, in the morning and then went to Ho to open the public water-electrification system there. So he found it politically feasible to visit here on the way. Right on time at 2:30 police sirens blared, the school children cheered on cue, and up drove the Rolls Royce. Because we were sweltering in suits, we were slightly dismayed to see that the Prime Minister wore an open-necked sport shirt and appeared more American than the Americans!

Our program of introductions and the meeting of local chiefs all went to the winds with his breezy informality, especially when the Adidome chief tried to monopolize him completely. One of his aides periodically yelled "Free-Dom," to which the crowd would respond "Free-Dom" while the PM grinned broadly. He seemed to like the hospital and appeared to be in no hurry. He is the kind of person who when he meets you acts as though he has just been introduced to a long-lost friend. He certainly makes a good impression, but looks much older than his pictures. His aides rushed him off promptly at 3:00, although we almost had him talked into coming here for "tea." We finally had to settle for some British newsmen who had gotten bored with politics and were more interested in mission philosophy, which was something relatively new to them.

We did manage to have some partying especially in Kenny's honor. Martha and Dr. Windisch had dinner with us and we had a big angel food cake. We talked Josephine into eating with us, but Tawia would have none of it. By that time Kenny was too tired to enjoy his toys much, but since then he has made good use of them.

The river has been falling the past week. The road, or what is left of it, is above water except where the big break is. We have now discovered that thirty feet of pipe were completely washed away. Our temporary pumping arrangement has worked well, but we'll have to figure out something new now that our pumping site is dry.

This morning at 6:00 a.m. Dick was awakened by a lusty shout of "Dr. Braun" coming from Dr. Windisch's chicken yard. When he woke enough to respond, she called: "I haf *hooge* snake here; won't you gif help?" By the time he got there, armed with a hoe, she had dispatched the snake and was beating it mercilessly while it coughed up her chicken eggs and finally a whole adult duck. It was a python, non-poisonous, a little over eight feet long, and five inches in diameter. Somebody in town will get a lot of shoes from that leather.

Tell Mrs. Whitcomb there is plenty of work waiting for her when she gets back. Neither Martha nor Trudy has found time to give a guiding hand to the Sunday school or Bible class for the hospital staff. Just trying to organize the nursing program of the hospital is a full-time job now.

✦ ✦ ✦

Adidome, Ghana
November 11, 1957

We are sorry you had to wait a long time for this letter. Whenever we try to write, something else has to be done, usually nighttime surgery. Yesterday, Sunday, we spent from 3:00 to 10:00 p.m. in the operating room doing three operations. In the last two weeks Dick has done two more Caesarean sections. Both babies are living, although one has a bad infection of the scalp and may die. The easiest way to do that operation, and the only way Dick has yet had the nerve to do it, is supposed to be absolutely contraindicated because of the increased danger of infection if the woman has been in labor more than six hours. The trouble is that our average patient does not get here until after forty-eight hours of labor and after the native midwives have performed all sorts of manipulations and have given strong medicine. So we are really quite lucky to save the mother, not to mention the baby.

This obstetric work is really discouraging sometimes. Almost none of the mothers come in early. In the new hospital we've had approximately a dozen deliveries. Of these we have had only four live babies and two of these have been from sections. Two of our operations last night were destructive operations on dead babies. One of the patients had been in labor four days. That is something almost never done in the States any more. But we get so many cases in which the baby is already dead that it is one of our common operations. Without the operation the mother would die. Even so, one of the mothers died last week. It would be discouraging if it were not for the few we can help to get good babies. They make up for all the rest. One of our first babies in the new hospital was a small premature baby less than three pounds. Its twin had died and it too was almost dead when the mother brought it here at the age of two weeks. We nursed it along over a month. Today the mother brought it back to clinic (she came to pay the last of her bill, and that in itself is amazing). The baby looked as healthy as any other normal eight-and-a-half-pound girl.

Last Wednesday Trudy, Josephine, and the boys piled into the station wagon with Dr. Windisch, her gardenboy, the driver, and stacks of boxes to drive to the nearest agricultural station in order to get seedlings and shrubs for the hospital grounds. After an hour and a half trip we finally arrived at the farm only to find that they had no seedlings or shrubs. But they did give us some cuttings that are now being carefully nursed along in the hope that a few may survive. Our long dry season has begun. This means that everything in the garden has to be watered twice a day or the dirt will turn to a dry powder. We had trouble with the first gardenboy we had here, so now we have a young Muslim who speaks Hausa and some Ewe. Since Trudy speaks English and some Ewe, she has to depend on the demonstration method to show him what needs to be done. Hamedo seems to be a good and willing worker, but not even his best efforts can keep the bugs off the melons.

On the way to the agricultural station we picked up your Christmas package at Sogankope. I had to open up the package because the clerk wanted to check customs. The clothes seem to be the right size and will be put away to make nice surprises at Christmas. The books from Aunt Gertrude are lovely and much appreciated. I put them away and give out one at a time. They are appreciated much more that way. Kenny likes the big Mother Goose. The toy box came from Texas too. Kenny likes the hexagonal cups that fit into each other and spends hours with them. He has not yet learned to put them on top of each other and build a pyramid. When one of his friends does that, he is much incensed because they do not do it right! They all have a good time with the big plastic ball. Although Kenny's friends are considerably older than he is, they like his toys because they have none of their own.

We will be thinking of you at Thanksgiving time. We will celebrate the day with a turkey dinner in the evening after the usual day of work at the hospital.

WE RECEIVED a letter from Webster Groves, Missouri, yesterday asking why we haven't answered previous questions and posing a few more that need urgent answers. The lack of answers is not entirely our fault. The letter in question was postmarked August 27. The trouble is that these Ghanaians are so intensely proud of their new country that they refuse to deliver any mail that does not have the name of their country on the envelope. We should however give the postal authorities credit for superior intelligence in finding Adidome in "West Africa," and also credit them with great magnanimity in stating simply, "Missent to Gambia."

Tonight we feel like sitting back and taking a deep breath. This has been a busy week, climaxed today by a jubilee marking the church's fiftieth year in Adidome. The early Bremen missionaries are reported to have made their first visit to Adidome a hundred years ago, but the first school and probably the first evangelistic effort date from 1907. These church celebrations, of which there have been several during the past few weeks, are a joyful meeting of the churches from surrounding areas. Last night lorries bringing choirs and congregations began arriving for the opening service. Yesterday the middle school had a sports day, something like a track meet, with students from Adidome and Mafi-Kumasi, located seventeen miles from here, competing. The athletes performed quite well considering their age and training. It was a real pleasure for Trudy to award the trophy to Adidome. Some enterprising people from town held a dance last night after the service and even imported a dance band from Ho for the occasion. This was not an official part of the jubilee by any means. But it was greatly enjoyed by most of the hospital people, townsfolk, and visitors as well.

When we first saw the program of speakers and anthems, we decided that the four of us here at the hospital would have to take turns going to the service. As it turned out, this is exactly what we did. Dick was there 10:00 a.m. to 3:00 p.m. The members of the congregation gathered at the church at 9:30, then marched in a procession to the cemetery for a memorial service, then back to the church for another four-hour service. They had a temporary palm-branch shelter for all the people overflowing the church (it has open sides). Dick was one of the ten speakers. He hopes he did not offend anyone by speaking only five minutes. We did enjoy the singing. Church choirs, singing bands, and school choruses from about eight towns participated. The church choir from Ho is really good. We are anticipating a trek to Ho with a recorder some time. The Adidome Middle School sang the "Hallelujah Chorus" in Ewe. When the service was finally over the hospital staff boys played the town team at football (soccer). It was a good game, although we lost 2 to 3.

I don't know whether the hospital game loss helped relations here or not. Things are a little strained at present. The townspeople think that since the hospital is in Adidome we should hire only local people. On the other hand, I know that some members of the staff here do act superior at times. Anyway the whole situation blew up last week when the local gendarmes started enforcing a bicycle license law that no one knew about. Four members of our staff were arrested, though no attempt was made to enforce the law in town. So Dick has been trying to straighten things out.

That is not our only trouble at present. Somebody has pocketed some of the hospital receipts. Now we are trying to check back over every patient and transaction for the past three months. The culprit will then be put on probation. If there are any more irregularities, he will be discharged.

It appears that we won't be homesick this Christmas. With the big International Missionary Council conference coming up in Accra the first week in January, there will be many guests. Dr. Wagner will be with us December 30 and 31. Then we must take him to Ho where he is to preach the New Year's Day sermon. For three days around Christmas, we will be entertaining Dr. Theodore Tucker, executive secretary of the Africa Committee of the National Council's Division of Foreign Missions, and Dr. Alford Carleton of the American Board of Commissioners for Foreign Missions. (Can you send some cranberries with him?)

Kenny is now speaking in sentences quite well. His vocabulary is multiplying rapidly, mostly because he mimics everything we say, even difficult technical words. One day last week he pilfered a pan from the kitchen, held it on his head, and announced to Trudy matter-of-factly, "Going to market." Next time she looked up he was one hundred yards down the road on the way to market. Dick put up a swing for him, so now the yard is attracting more children than ever. The Mosers spent two days of their vacation here last week. Kenny really enjoyed Danny and Janice. Even Kwame enjoyed all the activity. He stands up under the rough handling he gets from his brother very well; in fact, he likes it. He seems to make quite an impression around here because of his good health. Now when Dick tries to explain to a mother how to feed her baby, the interpreters automatically tell her about the fat baby at our house, who eats up to two bananas a day.

Our X-ray machine was installed since our last letter. So now Dick has another new job. He's also X-ray technician. We are still getting the darkroom fixed up, so there has not been much radiography yet. But already people are asking for it. Something mysterious like that machine must have great curative powers! The first chest film Dick took turned out well. He will have to learn all about it before he can teach someone else.

✐ ✐ ✐

Adidome, Ghana
December 5, 1957

IT SEEMS INCREDIBLE that it is only twenty days until Christmas. It feels like the middle of August. The only thing that looks seasonable is a gorgeous poinsettia tree in the village. We are going to Accra to do a bit of Christmas shopping but mainly to stock up on food for the many guests we expect to have during the next month or so. In this part of Ghana there doesn't seem to be much tradition centering around Christmas. We had thought that our guests could just observe the Christmas festivities. But when we told the pastor that we would have guests, he threw up his hands and asked, "What shall we do?" An extra church service is planned but that is about all. So now we are attempting to cook up some sort of Christmas nativity pageant or something in which the staff can participate.

We received a wonderful non-duty food package from Webster Groves on Monday. It is hard to say which things we appreciate most, for they are all wonderful ideas. Just a minute—the dried eggs are best of all ! What a boon to have eggs just at a time when we are ready to start our Christmas baking in the face of a local fresh eggs shortage. We are glad to have the instant dried potatoes, for sometimes potatoes are not to be had in Accra. Some of the nuts have already been used for cookies. We also received an announcement that a case of Folly Farm turkey is coming to us. Makes my mouth water already. Dr. Windisch promised us one of her fine ducks for the Christmas dinner when Dr. Carleton and Dr. Tucker will be with us.

Tomorrow is medical board meeting in Ho. Dick has prepared a statistical report which he hopes will bring some action. Our payroll has doubled, but actual patient attendance has fallen off. This is due in part to poor transportation factilities but mostly to the fact that the people here cannot pay. We have been trying to classify our patients according to income and find that 12 per cent of the patients earn less than $160 a year, and that 60 per cent earn between $160 and $280. At Worawora, however, 65 per cent earn more than $280. But all the educated people around here whom we have consulted maintain that in this area 40 per cent of the people earn less than $160. The only conclusion we can reach is that the poorer people cannot come to the hospital because they cannot pay. The average clinic payment has been ninety cents. This is comparable to a $16.00 payment for an office call by a person earning $3,000 a year at home. So patients who need care stay away. I hope the medical board has some suggestions. I fear they will not be too helpful; there is no money available.

We have a nice new piece of equipment exclusively for the

use of missionaries. The head of a nearby veterinary station asked for permission to dock his government outboard motor-boat at our landing. In return for this favor, he has said that we can use it whenever we wish. So now we will be able to go for a little spin up the river on Sunday afternoons.

In church this morning there were sixty-one baptisms and fifty-five confirmations in a service that lasted three hours. This occurred at Ho, where we stopped on the way to Accra. It was fun seeing Dolores Harkins and talking with her about you folks and conferences and camps at home.

⚹ ⚹ ⚹

Adidome, Ghana
December 14, 1957

WE KNOW all cards must be mailed before December 15 to ensure your getting them by Christmas. We hope you will get this. We wish you all a very merry Christmas. Our hearts will be with you at home as we unite to celebrate the birth of our Lord. We wish we could airmail Kenny and Kwame home to you for a couple of hours so grandparents and grandchildren could enjoy each other at Christmas. We will be looking forward to Christmas, 1959.

A week ago the whole family piled into the car and went to Ho where the medical board meeting was held on Saturday morning and afternoon. Dick presented the budget that Dr. Whitcomb had made out and it was approved. Worawora's budget had a planned deficit of 1,600 pounds and was sent back for reconsideration. Dr. Doering suggested that fees be raised to cut the deficit. But Dick suggested that fees be cut to make medical services available to more people of this area.

The board authorized Dick to make negotiations for clinics to be held in two outlying towns on the big market days. In this way we may be able to contact the people who cannot make the lorry trip to Adidome. We hope it will bring in a little money. Even more, we hope it will reach more people who need medical attention.

Trudy sat in at some of the meetings but was rather glad she had to leave to feed the children. It was a long-winded, tedious affair. Ruth Trost and Trudy debated whether to send over water and cookies at one o'clock, knowing that a little refreshment might give the board members energy to carry on without lunch. As it was, they met from ten o'clock in the morning to 4:30 in the afternoon without a break.

When you come to visit we'll make sure that you get a chance to attend church at Ho, for it is a wonderful experience. We are still marvelling at last Sunday's service there. We mentioned previously that at the morning service there were fifty-five infant baptisms, six adult baptisms, and fifty-five confirmations. For a while we wondered if the baptisms could keep up with the birth rate, for the babies just kept coming and coming. Some of these cute little ones were decked out in woolen bootees and woolen blankets (these were just for show, for the day was sweltering). There were anthems by the choir, the women's Bible class, the singing band, and the middle school. After the two and one half hour service, the singing band serenaded the confirmands. The whole group then paraded around the church grounds and the Mawuli campus. It was a real inspiration!

We left for Accra soon after dinner and arrived there in time for a brief swim in the ocean. This time Kenny was more interested in the sand than the sea. We thought this would be a more leisurely shopping trip, but as usual it turned out to be a wearing rush to get everything done by Wednesday noon. Our major purchase was a Gestetner duplicating machine for the mimeograph work of the hospital. Dick will have to learn how to use it. Then he will teach our stenographer in the office. We plan to send our next mimeographed letter from here so we can add personal notes to our friends.

Our living room is sporting a new maroon and gray fiber rug—Trudy's Christmas gift. Soon there will be curtains at the windows. We looked high and low for a tricycle for Kenny. They were $28.00. Finally the manager of the store said he had one in the basement that needed repairing. He let us have this one for $6.00. It lacks a front axle but we think we can rig one up.

The resthouse was pleasantly full this time. Walter Trost and Herb and Peggy Muenstermann were there. We had a pleasant visit with them and hope to see them again soon.

So far no missionaries here in Ghana have received a program of events for the International Missionary Conference. In fact, we heard that most of the meetings were for delegates only. So it is doubtful that we will get to meet some of the people who will be coming to Accra. We shall wait and see.

Sorry we have not been able to send you any pictures of the hospital at Adidome. All Dick's photography at the present time is confined to X-rays. We shall see what we can do when the VIPs are here. That term *VIP* seems to have been quickly adopted by the Ghanaians.

Preparing fu fu by pounding cassava in a giant size mortar with pestle

Community water faucets in village of Worawora provide good fresh water.

Chief at Ho and members of his official family; tribal affiliations are still important.

Seminary students at Peki doing their daily laundry

Y<small>OU HAVE BEEN</small> with us in thought very much the past few days. Even though we may be widely separated by distance, the joy of Christmas and the ever-increasing awareness of God's love bind us together. This Christmas has been different from any in our experience, but a very pleasant one nevertheless.

One of the best parts was having Dr. Alford Carleton as our guest. He fitted right into our household and was a very good standby for Grandpa. His fund of stories and his appearance remind us very much of Daddy Camp. He brought us a fine surprise too—cranberries. When Herb and Peggy Muenstermann delivered them to us before Dr. Carleton came we spent about ten minutes discussing the many delectable ways that we could use the cranberries. We spoke of relish, juice, pie, and sherbet. But we ended by making them all into relish because that makes us most nostalgic. Thanks so much for remembering our special liking.

Dr. Carleton arrived here on Monday morning just in time to exchange car and driver with the Muenstermanns who went to Worawora for Christmas after spending five days with us. We were hoping that they would stay for Christmas but their schedule of observing mission stations is rather tight and did not permit more time here. Our guests have been given the 75-cent tour of the Adidome station, which includes a tour of the hospital, a visit to the village on market day, a visit with the pastor, and an introduction to the paramount chief. Oh yes, and a motorboat ride on the river. They have also had a very adequate introduction to church services in Ghana. Herb preached the sermon last Sunday during the usual morning services, then in the afternoon we all went to communion. Following that the pastor, evangelist, presbyter, and two church mothers came out to pay him an official visit of welcome. They had an enjoyable time talking about the merits of church union. Yesterday Dr. Carleton preached the Christmas sermon, which was very fluently translated by the pastor.

The nativity play on Christmas Eve was something that all previous Christmas plays could not have prepared us for. The sensation of mid-July given by the very warm night was heightened by firecrackers and rockets that burst all around the shed church. The play was presented by members of the Bible class, who obviously enjoyed the drama. It began with a group of children and older girls dancing into the open church. Each succeeding act of the play was indicated by this "dancing curtain." Each incident of the nativity story was portrayed in great detail: the annunciation with an angel in flowing white cloths and so much chalk on her face that she could not be recognized; Joseph in the carpenter shop; Herod in his palace with a retinue of servants fanning him; Caesar's soldiers marching in motley array; Joseph and Mary on the way to Bethlehem (with an obviously tired Mary carrying a loaded basket on her head); Mary sweeping out the palm-leaf stable; the shepherds with a flock of plaintively baaa-ing boys; and so on to the hurried flight into Egypt. The crowd of children and curious adults watched the proceedings with great interest. But we wondered whether it was the dancing and the noise of the firecrackers outside that excited them or the story of the nativity.

Following the play, some of the nurses came back to the hospital and sang carols in the wards. A few of the patients woke up and appeared interested in the songs, while others slept. The patients were interested in the cards that were strung up in the wards for decoration. On Christmas morning Martha and a group of nurses had a service in the ward. Martha told the story of "Why the Chimes Rang," which was interpreted by our evangelist. Each patient was then given two pounds of rice and some candies and a small book of English words (some Golden books sent to us by Pilgrim Congregational Church in St. Louis).

Christmas afternoon seemed to us like a usual afternoon; there was an emergency operation. Since that did not take as long as we expected, Dick and Dr. Carleton managed to go into town to see the African dancing and drumming that had been planned as a reception for Dr. Carleton. In the evening our mission family finally had the traditional Christmas dinner featuring two of Dr. Windisch's ducks and Christmas pudding from a can. We opened our Christmas presents while seated around a small palm tree decorated with silver and gold balls and bright red tropical flowers. Kenny and Nathan received enough toys to last a year. Their little friends here like them even better. We greatly appreciate the gifts you sent.

Dr. Carleton says he would like to add a few lines:

"I am very happy to countersign this letter as a very grateful grandpa pro tem who has been taken into the family at Christmas time and who thoroughly enjoyed it! I need not tell you that Dick and Trudy are most excellent and most hospitable people (come out and give them a chance!), nor that Kenny and Kwame are two lively, normal, and very nice boys. I don't know when I have seen so much good nature, hours on end, as Kwame can exhibit; and Kenny is just at the age when he knows how to get into everything and (surprisingly) how to get out again! I have greatly enjoyed this Christmas at home with the Brauns."

—Alford Carleton

The plans for visits by both Braun and Camp grandparents is really exciting. We will start counting the days soon. To make the trip really worthwhile, we hope that you can stay longer than one month so you could get the feel of the work and the environment as well as have time to visit other stations.

✔ ✔ ✔

Adidome, Ghana
January 6, 1958

Happy New Year! We are a little late again, but that is because we're so busy. Dr. Windisch is on a two-week holiday in Accra. Dick has had to work quite a bit harder, but he is enjoying it thoroughly. The patient load has picked up a bit too and this makes us feel better. Dick has done two hernias and has two more scheduled. Today we had two deliveries—and two dead babies. One of these was tragic. The girl is a nurse (unqualified) in an Accra hospital but was home in a village nearby for maternity leave. When she did not deliver after some hours, she pleaded with the family to take her to a hospital. But they persisted with their midwives and native medicines until the baby was dead. When they finally brought her here she was in poor shape. For a while we thought we would not be able to save her, but now I think she will be all right.

Dick has just finished totaling the 1957 accounts. They balanced to within six shillings (out of 9,000 pounds), and that was surplus cash! Now we have to wait for Al Schwenke to come down here to audit them and show us how to get started for the new year. All these paper transactions of money are still confusing. As long as I get started in the right column I feel that I am doing well. We still have to prepare an annual report and then tackle the volumes of statistics that the government requires.

Dr. Wagner's visit here was rather short. He arrived on Monday evening and left Wednesday, New Year's morning, at 7:00 a.m. He made a few lucrative trips into town. We had cued the pastor that this was the *Fia Ga* (Big Chief!), so there was a special meeting of the congregation on Tuesday morning to present him with a beautifully woven kente cloth. Tawia estimated its value at about $80.00. Later the Adidome chief, not to be outdone, gave him another. He also bought three small ones to take back for gifts. At the watch-night service, he preached in competition with a dance about a hundred yards away.

On New Year's afternoon we finally got to go on the picnic we've been wanting for so long. Usually when we start planning a picnic we get emergency surgery. We took the boat about a mile upstream where we wanted to picnic on a sandbar. But after getting grounded fifty feet from the bar, we decided to go downstream to a higher bank. It was fun and we are looking forward to more picnics (and more emergency surgery!).

Last Saturday afternoon we had some excitement. Dick was awakened from a nap by a strange roar that turned out to be a grass fire just to the west of our land. We watched it apprehensively for almost an hour, wondering if it might come our way. We thought it would just burn itself out when it reached the river. But suddenly the wind changed. It raced toward us across a half-mile gap in about ten minutes. We quickly mobilized all the help available as fire-beaters and stood waiting for it at the edge of the clearing where we hoped we could beat it out as it slowed down for the short grass. It ruined what was left of our garden, burned out some of Whitcomb's shrubs, licked at our laundry, and would have taken Dr. Windisch's chicken house if we had not soaked it. In the end there was not too much damage done, but what was once beautiful grassland is now just ashes! The burnt smell will probably last for a long time. I don't know what we can do to stop fires. Burning is the time-honored method used here in clearing land for farming. I am told that this fire started in a piece of land disputed by two villages. Thus, if one village farms the land, those from the other village start fires on it. We are trying to get the chiefs to cooperate with us in settling this problem.

This is the season of the harmattan, which is a wind coming down from the Sahara bringing dust with it. So far we haven't noticed any gritty dust, but the haze in our otherwise clear atmosphere is very noticeable. The Africans complain that it's getting quite cold at night, but it just feels comfortably cool to us. The harmattan ushers in the long dry season that will last from now through March. We are trying to keep our growing things alive by watering them, but we won't try planting anything till the next rainy season.

Our Christmas mail is still coming in. The bulk of it arrived the week after Christmas—mostly newsy letters that we would like to answer personally. The books from Oak Park were much enjoyed. Our boys enjoy books of any kind. Kenny often follows us around the house carrying a book and saying,

"Read some." If we don't comply, he plops himself on the floor and proceeds to read in a loud voice, sometimes with the right phrases to go with the pictures. Kwame devours books too; but we have had to put a stop to that. It's too hard on the books. Kwame is now propelling himself over the floor by getting up on all fours and then falling forward (there's nothing backward about that). He is getting so wiggly that it's hard to hold him in church services.

Kenny speaks about Kwame Nkrumah too. He has probably listened to us discussing his recent unexpected marriage to an Egyptian girl. Our African friends tell us that this was a very astute political move that showed friendship to Egypt and Nasser and at the same time prevented tribal jealousies and feuding that would have arisen if he had chosen a girl from one of the major tribes of Ghana. Apparently the people would rather have a foreigner than a girl from rival people.

↙ ↙ ↙

Adidome, Ghana
January 11, 1958

WHILE I am stranded in the study, I'll make use of my enforced solitude with the typewriter by thanking you for some Christmas presents that just arrived today. By way of explanation, let me say that we usually keep the study locked and the key hung up high out of Kenny's reach so that he won't get in and wreak havoc. After getting him up from his nap and admiring our new presents, I stepped back in here to finish a birthday letter to Stephanie. Young son, finding that the key had been left in the door, turned it—naturally. I have asked

Kenny to get Hamedo, who is outside watering, but Ken doesn't seem to mind having Mommy out of sight as long as he knows where she is! Ha, help is coming now.

✦ ✦ ✦

Adidome, Ghana
January 16, 1958

WE'VE BEEN TO the mission meeting and back. A report of that should be coming in a few days. Dick is busy with annual reports for the government and I am trying to get grapefruit juice and pineapples canned before they spoil. On our way home from Worawora we bought seven dozen grapefruit and oranges for one cent each, and three nice pineapples for seventy-five cents. I am not convinced though that it really pays to can the fruit. The time involved and the expensive fuel are drawbacks. This will be a trial run.

Many thanks for the packages and the gift money. But the best gift of all will be to see you next September. How we are looking forward to that. We will save our vacation time for that so that we both can have time to enjoy being together. Your Christmas money will be saved for a special outing, perhaps a trip to the beach at Ada and dinner at the Ambassador when we feel the need for a change. Mr. Greig's check will be put in the general hospital fund. It will help cut expenses for patients.

Adidome, Ghana
January 22, 1958

WE RECEIVED Dad's letter from Cleveland admonishing us to write more often. At the same time we get letters from Oak Park complimenting us on our prolific letter-writing! Which brings us back to the old concept of relativity, especially of relatives.

I am having a hard time getting this letter moving because we are listening to the Hoffnung Music Festival for the first time. We just received the recording today. It is really magnificent. We are more sorry than ever now that we didn't get tickets for the original in London last year.

We spent January 12 to 14 in Worawora at our annual mission conference. All the missionaries of Ghana, except those on leave and two others, were there. We are certainly glad we are not living in Worawora now during the harmattan dry season. We didn't get a breath of fresh air in two days, and it was futile to try to stay clean. I think most of the dust was from the heavy lorry traffic on the nearby dirt roads rather than from the hot dusty wind from the Sahara as we had been led to believe. We stayed in Dr. Doering's guest room (he has the big house to himself now) while all the others stayed in the yet unopened surgical ward.

We are convinced again that we are not cut out for the life of repeated and protracted meetings. Dick's old conditioned reflex of somnolence in lectures or meetings (dating back to medical school days) promptly revived. He did wake up at the discussion of buying Adidome a new car, possibly a Mercedes diesel station wagon. Glory be, maybe we will be able to get rid of this rattly old contraption. We missed Chuck

Hein and his level-headed discussion at this meeting. He could not leave his seminary in Togo. But it was good to have Herb Muenstermann with us.

We have been keeping moderately busy since the first of the year. Our number of patients has shown some increase since that time. A few days ago we had both wards completely full (the private ward has still not been opened), but now many of those have gone home. We have had a couple of very critical medical patients in the last week. They have had a high fever, loss of consciousness, and, in the case of one, also jaundice and bleeding. So far we haven't figured them out—probably some sort of encephalitis, or maybe even yellow fever. They do not respond to any treatment we've been able to devise; but so far we haven't lost any. And they are slowly getting better. Last Saturday we had three normal deliveries, two of which were after long periods of labor. So Dick lost out almost completely on a night's sleep. Two years ago he never would have missed it; but now, being unused to it, it's hard to take.

We had to dismiss three members of our staff. There have been some hard words and some weeps; but the staff will be improved by it. One of the fellows has been here two years and has never done well. We could not risk putting him alone on the ward at night or in the evening. On the whole we think we now have a pretty good staff. We use quite a complete charting system, à la Barnes. It is beginning to look as though we may be transferred back to Worawora this summer when the Mosers go on furlough. Next January both Moser and Doering will be on leave. Perhaps a new doctor, Dick Biek, will be arriving before then. We hope some way can be found for us to stay here. This is home to us now!

The Friday before we left for the mission conference we had the last of our visitors from the International Missionary Conference: Dr. Pierce Beaver from the Federated Theological Schools of the University of Chicago, and a German professor of missions, a Dr. Hermeling, who spent a day with us. Dr. Windisch was so overjoyed to have a German guest that she took both of our visitors on the usual tour of the village. While there, they bought some kente cloth in the market. After that we managed to have the long-anticipated picnic on the river, with no emergency surgery to complicate things either! We found a fine place on a sand bar. That river really looks inviting for a swim; but we don't want to take the chance of getting schistosomiasis[5] (the name is bad enough), nor did we want to strike up too close an acquaintance with a crocodile.

We had a pleasant surprise in the garden the other day when we discovered that we have some good volunteer pineapple plants, two with baby pineapples. Tawia looked at one which was big enough to bear fruit and said, "The baby is dead." In Ewe the diminutive ending and the word for child is the same—*vi*. So you can speak about boys, little men, baby pineapples, or little pineapples and use the same ending. Anyhow its encouraging to see our garden produce something, even if we didn't plant it.

We will try to get caught up on personal letters as soon as the annual statistics are finished and Trudy has her sermon for Sunday and class outline on pharmacology planned.

---

[5] A disease caused by parasitic worms that infest the blood of humans.

THIS MUST BE another quickie in order to get it into the outgoing mail. We shall devote most of it to answering some of your questions. We now realize that some of our letters must have been lost. Perhaps they will show up now that the Christmas rush is over.

We did not get to attend any sessions of the International Missionary Conference for two reasons. Dr. Windisch wanted to take her leave then so she could get some refreshment for the mind as well as physical rest. She was able to attend some of the evening sessions open to the public (although the public was not invited to attend!). The joint communion service on New Year's Eve was a high point for her because representatives from all churches at the conference united for the sacrament. Dr. Beaver told us that the reason people were not invited was because the auditorium did not have a large capacity and there were no facilities to handle the overflowing crowds.

Nkrumah apparently made a good impression at the conference, speaking with sincere gratitude about the contribution that missionaries had made in the growth of this nation. As to Nkrumah's personal religious beliefs, we don't know. Whether his new wife is a Muslim or not (as you ask), we don't know. They were married in a civil ceremony only. He also seems very friendly to the Roman Catholics, making good speeches at their meetings too. In many ways tribalism, and to some extent nationalism, is bound up with the beliefs in tribal gods and fetishes. This means that a repudiation of paganism might be viewed as a repudiation of tribal loyalties and the tribal system of government. Ghana is making rapid strides but is not ready to give up chiefs and tribal loyalties.

We received Dr. Wagner's report on his African tour yesterday. It certainly is extensive. He was able to learn some things about church organization and management that we did not know.

Mom Braun, let us know what colors of kente cloth you want for a chair covering. I think we can have some made here. It is cheaper here than at Ho or elsewhere. Kente cloth is expensive; but when you consider the hours spent in weaving, it is reasonable. It would be excellent for draperies because it is colorfast and wears like iron. Dr. Wagner's cloth was an immense piece of material, measuring six feet by twelve feet and made up of long strips four inches wide. There were strips of gold thread woven in and a nice border. It is a fine example of true Ghanaian craft. We hope he will use it on occasion and not relegate it to a souvenir closet. I want to talk to the local weavers about making place mats.

You can buy little carved elephants of ivory quite reasonably, but most of the carved things come from Nigeria. The hand-carved sandalwood box we sent you for Christmas may have originally come from India. The inlaid material is mother-of-pearl. We bought it from a Hausa trader. We are glad you like it. Martha picked up four packages for us in Sogankope. They really charged her plenty for duty. One of the packages was jars of turkey products from Uncle Edward —not one jar broken. The glasses will be treasured for drinking glasses in this thirsty country.

Yes, we can use your old Christmas cards for souvenirs and instruction cards for our patients. Stanley Wilke has listed our address as one place to send packages of cards. Yes, we would appreciate old picture magazines for our patients to look at and for the nurses to read during time off at home. Copies of the *Reader's Digest* are covered thoroughly by those who can read English. *Youth* magazines are fine. If the magazines are sent one or two at a time by slow book rate mail, they will be delivered in Adidome and not entail a trip to Sogankope.

⚹ ⚹ ⚹

Adidome, Ghana
February 6, 1958

I<small>T IS HARD</small> for us to imagine your venturing out in the snow and ice while we are in the midst of one of our warmest seasons. The temperature ranges from about 75 degrees in the early morning to 95 degrees at noon. But it's not at all uncomfortable in our breezy house. I guess it shows that we are acclimated now. A seed catalogue came in the mail this week. How I would love to go through it and order a lot of seeds. But it is not the time to plant. And neither of us has the time to supervise the gardenboy in the planting of a flower garden.

For the last two weeks we have had Mabel Burket as our house guest. Around Christmas she had a case of dengue fever followed by a siege with the flu. She has a difficult time recuperating in Worawora because she feels guilty leaving the work to the other two nurses while she rests. The only solution was to get her away from there. I am sure she has the proper rest here because there is nothing for her to do but read, talk, and go on an occasional picnic. She and Martha went to Accra for a couple of days to see the doctor and to go shopping. They came back Tuesday because the resthouse was overflowing with people. The Desmonds had just arrived from furlough with their four children all under six. And the Youngs came on the same boat. Mr. Young is the new business manager for Worawora.

Probably the Youngs will be here for a few days next week on their tour of the mission stations. We hope Mr. Young can be persuaded to come here a few days a month to conduct our business. Dick isn't having any trouble keeping books or making them balance, but it would be a help to have someone who does it right! He would probably save us money! But I guess he's needed even more in Worawora.

After a New Year's surge of patients, the number has dropped. It's been a bit dull the last week without even an emergency operation to liven things up. We have had some pretty sick patients and a distressing number of deaths. Right now we have a big, strapping young fellow very ill with tetanus, which he apparently contracted from guinea worm infection. Two outlying clinics will be started next week at villages twenty miles from here. Dr. Windisch will spend two days a week there.

A few weeks ago on the way to Worawora, about fifteen miles from here, we saw some baboons crossing the road ahead of us. There must have been at least thirty, each weighing between forty and fifty pounds. Many of them stopped and climbed small trees in order to get a better look at us. That is the first wildlife we have seen, besides snakes. Dick got a small fright from a snake last week. He got in a patient with a severe snake bite six days old. He asked if they had caught the snake and asked for a description of it in order to facilitate treatment. A few days later one of the relatives announced that he had the snake and would show it to him. Dick eagerly took the lid off the paint can. It was then that he learned that the snake was very much alive. It was a small adder, only about a foot long, but the most dangerous kind around here. They had not killed it because one of the local fetishes is that if the snake is killed, the patient will also die. But they had no objection when Dr. Windisch killed it. I am sure they thought merely that our fetish was stronger than theirs.

The other day we heard a loud cracking sound, like someone breaking wood. We thought some women were out in the bush chopping wood, but then we discovered that seed pods on a tree in our front yard were cracking in the bright sun and falling to the ground. This morning we discovered purple flowers like wisteria on that very tree.

We finally have a report on the bacteriological testing of nine water samples taken at two different times from our taps. All are sterile. So it looks like our new purification plant is pretty effective in cleaning the dirty river water (although the cost of running it is about twenty cents per 1,000 gallons). So we are starting to take the water right out of the taps without boiling it.

Last week we had an informal game night for the staff, using the African game Adi, the Korean game Yoot, and Pit. The last-named was by far the most popular. So much shouting and laughing we have not heard for a long time. Now we are planning a Valentine's Day party. The only problem is that the girls are so terribly outnumbered.

Another slow boat from New Orleans arrived at Takoradi, bringing a *Messenger*, a flock of Christmas cards, your calendar, and other interesting things.

HAPPY Valentine's Day to each of you! It did not occur to us
that today was the day for cupids and arrows and hearts until
yesterday when Trudy inadvertently suggested a Halloween
party. But we did have cupcakes with pink icing this noon to
remind us of the season.

Whenever things seem quiet in any kind of medical institution, the staff soon has a peculiar feeling that something's
about to happen. It always happened that way in Maternity
Hospital just before we were swamped with babies. And it
happened that way too in the Indianapolis General Emergency room just before a big accident. It happens here too.
On Saturday morning things were so quiet that Trudy decided
to clean out the storeroom, which was a real mess. Martha
was planning to get some washing done, and Dick was going
to work in the study. Then just in time for dinner our new
missionary business manager for Worawora hospital drove in
with his wife and six-year-old daughter (it's lucky spaghetti
is extendable).

The Youngs were very congenial house guests over the
weekend. We gave them the 75-cent tour of the hospital. Then
on Saturday afternoon we had a picnic down at the riverside.
We were not able to go over to our favorite sandbar because
the motor for the boat had not been fixed and the boat is too
heavy to handle with the small native oars. We hope we will
be able to fix the motor today.

The Youngs come from St. Marys, Ohio, where Russ (Mr.
Young) had been teaching for three years. He spent some
time in the army, and after that majored in business and eco-

nomics at Heidelberg College. It will be a real asset to Worawora to have him manage the books and the buying.

Alice Moser is especially relieved. She has been keeping all
the books and is eager to retire because she is expecting the
third little Moser in March and has to begin packing for
furlough in mid-May. There is plenty of work for any willing
person in Worawora, so Jean Young will probably find herself
involved in mission work as well as being responsible for
teaching her daughter Kathy. We are hoping that as Russ
works into his job he will be able to purchase for both hospitals, thus saving time and money with big orders.

Our premonition that something was going to happen surely
came true on Sunday. Dick had quite a difficult delivery on
Sunday morning. Then on Sunday afternoon another woman
came in labor, but this one with a ruptured uterus. At first
Dick was not able to determine for sure whether the uterus
was ruptured, but after the dead child was delivered it became certain that it was. For this the only treatment was
surgery. This was the first hysterectomy Dick ever did. And
he had not even seen a hysterectomy for ruptured uterus. But
he sweated through it. Miraculously, the woman is doing well
and has not even required much medication for pain. Sometimes it is difficult for us to say that we have really saved a
life or done something that a little patience would not heal by
itself. But this time we can say that our being able to help
actually saved this woman's life.

At first we were overawed by the idea of living in a seven-
room house; but last week when the Youngs and Mabel Burket
were our house guests we realized the advantages and fun of
having plenty of room for everyone. Mabel is feeling much

more rested and will probably return to Worawora next Monday.

We got the lovely picture of "Christ and the Children." We shall have it framed for our living room.

⏥ ⏥ ⏥

Adidome, Ghana
February 21, 1958

THIS HAS BEEN another busy week, the kind we like to see once in a while but also the kind that makes us glad when it's over. It's strange how our surgery comes in waves. The first week in January we had a lot, and then for a while almost none. We should have known last week that the hysterectomy we struggled through would probably be the start of something. Incidentally, that patient is still alive and making a slow recovery. With all the things that might have gone wrong with her (and still may), we are just grateful that she is improving at all. So far this week we have done four hernias—one today on a year-old child. We also did an intestinal resection. The man who had that operation came in about last Thursday with intestinal obstruction, very dehydrated, but with no externally visible cause of the obstruction (such as incarcerated hernia). Our poor X-ray technique did not help much. He was in no shape to operate, so we just gave him intravenous fluids. By Monday he was in better general condition, but still just as obstructed. So finally we decided to operate. That's another one we really sweated over. We resected about a foot of gangrenous intestine. His condition was caused by an internal hernia and his entire abdomen was filled with infection and contamination from the perforated intestine. He

⏥ 143

has not yet started to improve and now we are down to our last three bottles of intravenous fluids (he's used about $20.00 worth already). If he isn't able to take food by tomorrow or the next day I'm afraid he's doomed. And now we have a D&C[6] scheduled for tomorrow and a Caesarean section and three hernias scheduled for next week. I wish this surgery would spread itself out a bit. It will be fun when Dr. Whitcomb comes back.

Dr. Windisch has started her visits to outlying clinics two days a week in two towns about twenty miles away. She has been authorized by the mission to develop the program as she wishes, so she has plans of making it a six-day-a-week affair. So far the clinics have done well. One day about seventy patients showed up. Apparently this takes care of the patients who could never, or would never, come to the hospital. She takes along a clerk, interpreter, dispenser, and driver.

We had another grass fire this week. This time it came from a village in the south and was fanned by a stiff breeze. We had everyone we could find, posted at the cut grass ready to beat it out when it reached there. But the grass was so dry and the wind so strong that it raced right on through even though the grass was only six inches high. It killed two or three dozen of our young fruit trees and would have burned a crippled old man who was walking up the road to the hospital if Dick and a nurse had not run out and carried him to safety. Even the chief seems to be powerless to put an end to clearing land by fire. I don't know what we can do about it. Perhaps one good result of the fire is that it chased a few snakes out of the bush. Two were killed this time, one a rather

---

[6] A dilatation and curettage operation.

deadly adder and the other a non-poisonous but still rather dangerous boa. The latter was eight inches in diameter and fourteen feet, eight inches long. One of our laborers, a little guy, had the courage to approach it armed only with a cutlass. He killed it too—after the others ran away. But it had been burned by the fire and was pretty weak. It was a good thing to have that one killed because she had about thirty eggs inside of her. We were careful to see that the eggs were buried; otherwise they might hatch in the bright sun.

Last night (it is now Saturday morning), the women's Bible class presented their meeting for the World Day of Prayer. They had been practicing the hymns and responses at their weekly meetings since the beginning of the year. Each of the women who was able to read led in some part of the program such as the litany, prayer, or meditation. And those who cannot read Ewe, including Trudy, offered a prayer. The fellowship of Christians is very real at a time like that when people all over the world are uniting in prayer at the same time. We are very fortunate in this church to have several women who are able to furnish good leadership in the Bible study group. Certainly Trudy is not able to do it when hospital duties so often keep her from class.

You ask about a shirt for Tawia. Get a small size in men's short-sleeved shirt—something that looks typically American. A bright plaid or bright design and color would certainly please him.

This week we made some root beer using root beer extract that Mrs. Whitcomb brought along but never used. It was a bit hard to get the gelatinous stuff to dissolve but it does make a pretty good drink. The yeast acts very quickly in this climate so we have to tie the corks on very securely. Even then, they really pop off when the string is cut. Perhaps you could find more root beer extract to send.

✗ ✗ ✗

JUST AS I was sitting down to write this letter, the Adidome lorry arrived bringing our new (for us—really, second-hand) operating table. By that time it was nine o'clock at night, so we had to enlist help from some of the employees who live on the hospital grounds. They helped move the crate from the truck to the ground. The thing must weigh at least a ton. It took seven strong fellows to shove it onto the ground. We wonder how they managed to unload it at Accra harbor where all freight must be brought in on small skiffs manned by young Africans. Now it is outside the operating room waiting for Dick to come home from Accra to unpack it. Martha and I don't want the responsibility of handling that mighty expensive piece of equipment. Jonathan, our African in charge of surgery, said we should initiate it with some important piece of major surgery like a Caesarean. Hope we don't.

Dick went to Accra on Wednesday to do a lot of hospital buying. He took the Chevy carry-all so he could take a load of empty coke cases, some bottled gas tanks, and sundry other things. Tawia went along to wash dishes for Dick and to sit in the car guarding purchases while Dick does the shopping.

Martha and I were almost glad to see Dick leave for a while because he kept us hopping recently, doing at least one piece of major surgery every day for the last week and a half. We had a run of hernia operations back in January, then a lull, and another run last week. On Monday we had our first scheduled Caesarean section. All the rest have been emergencies. It had been postponed for more than a week until the woman's husband could be present. We were very happy that the child turned out to be a perfect little girl, for the woman had lost three or four children during delivery before. Even while Dick was in surgery, a young girl with acute typhoid fever (we think) went into shock and all our best efforts were unable to save her.

That evening Dick and I presided at a very difficult delivery that kept us burning the lights longer than usual. During that delivery, a young boy who had fallen off the top of the Adidome lorry was brought in unconscious. He reeked so of alcohol that we could not be sure whether his symptoms were due to drunkenness or brain injury or both. He improved very much on Tuesday and was up walking around, against doctor's orders. But on Wednesday he lost consciousness and died. Only drastic brain surgery on Monday night could have saved him. Next morning we were called out early to help a woman whom the native midwives had given up. The baby was already dead and we were afraid we'd lose the mother too, but now she's making a good recovery. The final blow came yesterday when a month-old baby that Martha had literally been breathing life into, finally gave up the struggle. It's been quite a week. We won't mind if things get a bit dull now so we can write letters and can lemon juice.

At times like these we really appreciate our children for the entertainment and diversion they give. They are pretty good sports when you consider that both Mommy and Daddy are away all day. But frankly, none of us likes it too well. Kenny has now learned to ride his Christmas tricycle and is quite skillful about steering around on the veranda. I was beginning to wonder if the tricycle would be worn out by Kenny's playmates before he learned how to make it go.

Dick's birthday did not get much attention, but we did celebrate by opening a jar of Folly Farm turkey and by putting candles on a pecan pie made from nuts that Martha's mother sent her. Since lemons have just come back on the market, I guess a lemon chiffon pie will be ordered for Sunday.

Our long dry spell of no rain for well over a month was broken on Tuesday by a good drenching rain. How we wish it had come a week earlier to put out that devastating grass fire. Dick counted over three dozen of our grafted fruit trees that were killed or severely damaged. The bananas will pull through, we hope, but the citrus trees are doomed.

This is the first letter in many weeks that I have written in entirety. Both of us usually write several paragraphs, sometimes taking over for the other in the midst of a paragraph. Dick usually starts the letter while I'm making evening rounds and then I finish it the next morning and give it to one of the boys to take to the post office.

✦ ✦ ✦

Adidome, Ghana
March 3, 1958

CROCUSES blooming? In our perennial summer it is easy to get nostalgic about spring and the excitement of watching things start to bloom again. The rainy season will begin soon. Then all the farmers will be busy on their "farms," which are actually plots about an acre in size. Before the rains begin there is a very strong dry wind that would scorch any young plants, so we have to wait with our planting.

When we come home on furlough we hope to bring some of the fine cloths made in this vicinity. The material is woven into strips about four to six inches wide because the weavers do not actually have looms and are forced to tie the threads to a tree or fasten them with heavy rock. Using these crude methods, they cannot manage very many threads at one time. Considering this, some of the weaving is remarkable. When the strips are finished, they are sewn together into a larger cloth. Some kente cloths cost as much as thirty pounds ($84.00). The woven cloths are highly treasured and passed down in the family, usually from uncle to nephew and according to ancient inheritance customs. At first we were surprised to learn that this was the way a person's wealth was invested. But when you think about it, this makes as much sense as investing one's wealth in diamonds, which are not nearly as practical.

You would be interested to see the work of the goldsmiths here. They do very intricate work, specializing in the making of earrings and golden chains for women. The gold has a bright yellow—almost orange—appearance. It looks almost like copper. I wonder what the metallic composition is. Almost every village has one or two goldsmiths. One would think there isn't enough business to make a living. But gold earrings are treasured here just as cloths are. A woman will often save all her pennies to buy a nice pair.

THE DRY SEASON ought to be over soon. We've been having strong winds again that make us keep doors and windows closed. When the wind blows it's almost cold; but when the wind stops, it's very hot. Nothing like variety! There has been quite a bit of rain around us, but none here. Fires have come to the hospital from every side. We don't even make much attempt to put them out now. Some of the burnt banana and coconut trees are reviving, but not the citrus trees.

Trudy kept her eyes open for the advent of the first limes of the season. She gave a shilling to each of a number of friends in town and asked them to buy limes when they saw them. So came last Friday—well, the season is really here. For those four shillings we have over a bushel of limes lying all over the house. So we drink limeade instead of ordinary water, and eat lime sherbet, lime chiffon pie, and so on. Just call us limeys. We are not complaining though. For the first time we are far enough ahead in our supply so we can bottle some lime juice for dry days ahead.

Last Thursday was the first anniversary of Ghana's independence. It was also the first anniversary of our arrival in Ghana. The time certainly has gone fast in some ways, although we are so much at home that in other ways we feel as if we've lived here all our lives. The anniversary of Ghana's independence was celebrated in a big way here. When Dick was in Accra two weeks ago, he saw all the decorations going up just as they were last year. Kwame Nkrumah's statue was waiting to be unveiled. The country came in for a good deal of complimentary congratulatory messages from all over the world, probably on the whole justly deserved. The new country has done pretty well by itself for the first year and is about as stable economically and politically as anyone could have hoped for. Now we see that the prime minister is going to the States in July for a state visit. It will be interesting to follow his reception.

We went to Ho on Thursday for a special missions conference. It was a good chance to get together with the others again. With the Desmonds back, there certainly is a mob of children. There were twelve there, with six absent. Alice Moser is expecting her new one anytime now. The Mosers are leaving on furlough in May; then I fear we will have to leave Adidome and move to Worawora. The hospital has been a little quieter this past week. We had only a few operations and a workable number of outpatients. We've continued to have the wards pretty full, usually about thirty-two or thirty-four, but still not up to the full capacity of forty-eight.

It's Tuesday morning now. This is Trudy taking over on the typewriter. The presence of two small boys in the study is certainly not conducive to coherent thought. Kenny is very interested in the typewriter and keeps chanting N, O, A as he looks at the keys. He has been sticking close to me for the past few days because I've kept sticking close to Kwame. The baby has been under the weather with some undetermined kind of fever. He seems better today, but not quite up to his cheerful buoyant self.

On Sunday the women's Bible class walked out to the hospital to attend the Sunday service for the patients. Afterward they came over to our house for a brief meeting and something to drink. I was going to serve tea but I was unable to because the tea was all molding. The substitute was lemonade, which they all dutifully drank. But I heard one woman whisper in Ewe, "There's medicine in it." Another said to me, "Thank you for the drink. This is good for malaria, isn't it?" What strange people we Americans are, drinking lemonade by the quart.

⚹ ⚹ ⚹

Adidome, Ghana
March 17, 1958

At last the dry season appears to be virtually over. We had two good rains and they really changed the atmosphere. The air, after four months of dusty haze, is again clear and the sky is beautifully colored. Things started to grow all of a sudden. Each field has sprung up with small lily-like flowers that bloom mostly at night and then suddenly disappear. Clinic attendance has taken a sharp drop as the Africans start their "farms."

The local veterinary station has finally repaired the outboard motor and we have been making good use of it the last two Sundays. On both occasions we took a couple of the African nurses along. We like to stop along the river at little villages that are inaccessible except by boat. Our visits always arouse considerable excitement, especially among the children who crowd around us. Quite frequently we strike terror into some of them who have obviously never seen a *yevu* (white man). The adults seem to be genuinely appreciative of our visits. And of course we always have to make a "state visit" to pay our respects to the chief. So it is impossible just to take a stroll through town. These villages are much more primitive and "typical" (in the sense of our stereotypes) than Adidome. A fishing village just across the river from us, Bakpa, is really a beautiful place with grass huts lining the high river banks and coconut palms offering ample shade.

You ask about eye surgery. That's a specialized field we shall leave for Doc Whitcomb, since Dick knows nothing about eyes. Our cases recently have been mostly medical, including some tough cardiacs. A local fetish priestess, who has been responding quite warmly to our evangelist's efforts, has not responded well at all to our medicines. So far we have had only one case of meningitis, one of the most dread epidemic diseases in Ghana. After a critical week the patient—a young boy—is making a good recovery.

Much love to all of you, from

Dick, Trudy, Kenny, and Kwame

Editor's Note

These letters have reached an end, but hardly a conclusion. There have been many other letters since these, and new chapters in the ministry of healing are still being written by Dr. and Mrs. Braun. It seems especially fitting that the last letter above should end on a rising note. In the face of meningitis, one of the dread epidemic diseases in Ghana, the authors report that "the patient—a young boy—is making a good recovery."

In the meantime, great happiness has come to this young couple through the birth of their third son, Alan Richard. Following a short study furlough in the United States, the Brauns plan to take up their work as Christian missionaries in Ghana. Thus the reader can well imagine that the future promises more challenging opportunities to test the nerve and try the spirit of this courageous team of medical missionaries. From the events that have marched across the pages of the foregoing letters, it is not difficult to conclude that such a future will prove agreeable to the Brauns, who by this time have amply demonstrated that their concern is to serve their fellow men in Ghana in the spirit of the Master.